MW00442162

POWER TRAINING
IN KUNG-FU AND KARATE
by Ron Marchini and Leo Fong

© Ohara Publications, Incorporated 1974
All rights reserved
Printed in the United States of America
Library of Congress Catalog Card Number: 74-14128

Twenty-first printing 1996

ISBN-0-89750-047-4

GRAPHIC DESIGN BY DAVID P. KAPLAN

WARNING

This book is presented only as a means of preserving a unique aspect of the heritage of the martial arts. Neither Ohara Publications nor the author makes any representation, warranty or guarantee that the techniques described or illustrated in this book will be safe or effective in any self-defense situation or otherwise. You may be injured if you apply or train in the techniques of self-defense illustrated in this book, and neither Ohara Publications nor the author is responsible for any such injury that may result. It is essential that you consult a physician regarding whether or not to attempt any technique described in this book. Specific self-defense responses illustrated in this book may not be justified in any particular situation in view of all of the circumstances or under the applicable federal, state or local law. Neither Ohara Publications nor the author makes any representation or warranty regarding the legality or appropriateness of any technique mentioned in this book.

OHARA ▯ PUBLICATIONS, INCORPORATED

SANTA CLARITA, CALIFORNIA

ACKNOWLEDGEMENT

Our special appreciation to Richard Tutt II for the photography and to Marvin Langford, for his willingness to pose for the technique section of this book.

DEDICATION

To our wives, Jo Anne Marchini and Libertad Sangalang Fong, whose encouragements and support have made the completion of this volume possible. And to our parents whose interest in good health have made us more appreciative of the value of exercising and good nutrition. And to those instructors and colleagues in karate and weight lifting who have contributed to the authors' knowledge through the years.

FOREWORD
By Dr. Ted Frigard

Ron Marchini and Leo Fong are pioneers. Pioneering is never easy and is a very lonely path which few have the courage to travel. Both men are proficient in their respective arts of karate and kung-fu, but their outstanding attributes lie in what they are doing for others. They are influencing and changing the lives of those they teach.

Fong and Marchini have not only enriched, but actually changed our lives through karate. Tuesday and Thursday evenings always meant excitement in our home. These were the nights when my four children and I attended the Marchini-Fong karate school. It was a marvelous experience, for it brought our family closer together. We soon discovered that karate was more than self-defense. It is a philosophy and a new way of life which teaches self-discipline.

I watched my children develop self-confidence. They seemed to expel their hostilities while exercising, which improved their disposition and manners. Through karate, they became more aware of their potentials in other areas of life. My youngest son, Marc, began to move with more self-assurance as his coordination improved and his inner confidence developed.

Lance wanted to learn karate for self-defense, mainly because he was antagonized by bigger schoolmates. As his confidence increased, it began to project itself into other sports. Lance played on a little league baseball team, school soccer team, and track team.

He later won trophies in golf and tennis. Marchini and Fong encouraged him to enter the junior division of the Captain Weber Days Karate Tournament, which attracted participants from all over California. I was hesitant about allowing him to compete, as he was small for his age and was at the bottom of his age division.

He promptly won five matches and reached the finals, barely losing the championship in a sudden-death overtime contest.

I was very proud of his improvement, which came with only one year of training. Incidentally, the bigger boys at his school do not send him home crying any longer. In fact, karate has developed his self-confidence and self-discipline to a point where others need no proof of his fighting potential.

Karate was misunderstood for years and, as a result, was not widely accepted. Today, it has not only become an acceptable art, but an admirable one as well.

If there is to be any hope for a generation which has grown rotund, now more than ever, the virtue of self-discipline is needed for eating and exercise. Simply, our society has become affluent, and the symbol of affluence is the paunch.

Fong and Marchini have devoted their lives to studying the martial arts, exercise, nutrition and health. They have personally used these techniques successfully and now wish to share their knowledge with you.

This book was written to focus your attention on the wisdom of correct nutrition and exercise. Alert men and women, the advanced thinkers, the doers, the successful and dynamic people everywhere are beginning to treat their bodies as carefully as they treat their minds.

In the long run, the healthy habits espoused in this book will save money which would normally be spent on trips to the doctor's office, for the dedicated authors have laid down the stepping stones toward adding years to life and life to years.

PREFACE

In the last twenty years, weight training has revolutionized the sports world. Records in track, baseball, football, judo, swimming, golf and many other sports are cases in point. Weight training has played an integral part in improving the performance of the modern athlete. The athlete of today is much stronger and faster than his counterpart of yesteryear when systematic weight training was not accessible.

Today, barbells, dumbbells and other similar equipment are found on every high school and college campus. Many colleges offer weight training as an accredited elective course. It's estimated that more than 3500 body builders and weight lifters compete regularly in contests throughout the United States. Another two to three million train with weights at home, YMCAs, health clubs and other facilities where equipment is available.

Since the advent of the martial arts in the U.S., there has been much confusion and controversy over the value of weight training as a supplement to the budoka's traditional training program.

In an interview conducted by BLACK BELT MAGAZINE in 1970, seven prominent martial artists expressed their opinions on weight training as applied to their fields. These opinions varied from suggesting only moderate use of weights to advocating total abstinence from them. All agreed that power plays an important role in the practice of the various martial arts, but they differed on the ways of developing that power. Only one man stated that every martial artist should include weight training as a regular part of his program. Some claimed that weight training retards speed, stifles gracefulness and makes the practitioner muscle-bound. One of the interviewees even suggested that weight training may cause serious injury to body joints.

Although the modern athlete is a prime example of the effects weight lifting can have on performance, many laymen still believe those who work with weights become overblown, clumsy and slow. It is the purpose of this book to present to the serious martial artist the positive aspects of weight training. The authors have a combined total of twenty-one years spent in practicing the martial arts, and each has found weight training an integral and indispensable part of his training program.

One common misconception surrounding weight training is that it retards speed. Many people associate weight training with a muscle-bound condition. By muscle-bound, we assume the term refers to a general slowing down of the contraction speed of the muscular system. Perhaps the muscle-bound myth stems from the impressions created by professional strong men who toured the country around the turn of the century. They were large boned and heavy around the midsection. Their weight lifting activities coupled with a large consumption of food naturally made them even larger and heavier. Due to this image, it was quite easy to assume weight lifting makes one overblown and slow. However, there is no scientific evidence which lends credit to these beliefs. On the contrary, latest research has shown weight training, coupled with stretching exercises, increases the speed of muscular contraction.

Many practitioners of the martial arts have deprived themselves of an opportunity to reach their maximum peak through weight training because of their fear of becoming muscle-bound. But there are other factors to consider as well. Research has shown that very few have the skeletal and body structure to become a potential "Mr. America". This is particularly true of those in the martial arts. Participants in the martial arts are usually small boned and possess small, wiry builds designed for efficiency rather than muscularity. However, weight training will increase strength in a devotee regardless of his build. The belief that every person who trains with weights will become a subject for a body building magazine is illusory.

Another common misconception asserts that the weight

trainer's muscles will turn to fat when he quits training. This contention is based on a misunderstanding of the function of the muscular system. Muscles are composed of protein and protein does not turn into fat. A muscle will become soft from inactivity, but will not gain in size after physical exercises are discontinued unless the person consumes more carbohydrates than he is able to use up. A systematic weight training program gives the body general muscle tone, resulting in the strengthening and hardening of the muscle fibers. Once exercise ceases, the muscles lose their hardness and become soft.

Interviews with body builders and weight lifters who have discontinued their training have revealed that those lifters who are heavy before training tend to become overweight when they quit; particularly if they are not careful about their food intake. On the other hand, those who are thin to begin with tend to return to that shape after they quit training.

A third misconception is that weight training does nothing to develop cardiac endurance and enlarges the heart. In a recent investigation concerning the effect of weight lifting on the heart, two graduate students from the Exercise Physiology Laboratory at Florida State University found weight training *can* develop cardiac endurance. The subjects of the experiment were forty advanced and novice weight lifters and body builders who were tested during their regular one-hour workouts. The number of heartbeats per minute were recorded during and after each subject's exercise. During the workout, the average heartbeat rate for all subjects was 152 beats per minute, while the normal rate ranged from 60 to 72 beats per minute. Between exercises, the heart rate gradually decreased to an average of 120 beats per minute. In other words, during a normal weight lifting workout, the heart rate varied up to 32 beats per minute.

This 32 beat difference represents the condition of the heart, and an athlete who is in top physical condition will have a lower heartbeat than someone who is out of shape. Hence, there is good reason to believe that weight lifting has a beneficial effect on the body's most vital muscle, the heart.

In another study, ten advanced lifters were tested on several physiological measures during and after two sets of high repetition squats. The average heart rate during exercise for all subjects was 186 beats per minute. The conclusion reached after the experiment was that weight training can and does develop cardiac endurance. Through weight lifting exercises, the vascular system slows the heart beat and the blood pressure, and as a result, the weight trained person is able to work longer and perform more difficult movements in advanced exercises without undue fatigue.

One common myth among the anti-weight training advocates says weight training will give the subject an enlarged heart. Weight training will stretch the heart muscles. This is very important because a flexible heart trained to work progressively against the principle of 'overload' can work far more efficiently and comfortably, and for longer periods of time at lower levels of thrust. Research has shown that when the heart muscle is thickened as well as stretched, it can pump more blood per minute through the body with much longer "at rest" intervals between beats. This would obviously lengthen the life of one's heart, and consequently his life span.

In view of these discoveries by experts in the field, it is our feeling that weight training can only benefit anyone who includes it in their regular training program, particularly the serious karateka who seeks to develop greater power in the delivery of techniques.

ABOUT THE
AUTHORS

RON MARCHINI

Ron Marchini was born on March 4, 1945 in Stockton, California. He attended local schools and was active in swimming, football and baseball at Lincoln High School. While attending junior high school, Mr. Marchini took an active interest in weight lifting and has remained with it ever since. He has an Associate of Arts degree from San Joaquin Delta College and a Bachelor of Arts degree from the University of the Pacific, where he majored in physical education and minored in sociology.

Marchini's martial arts training began in 1964 when he took his first lesson in karate under Gordon Kennedy, a rembukai black belt. Serving in the Army under the six month program, he became a drill sergeant and gave hand to hand combat instruction. Following his active tour of duty, Mr. Marchini was employed by the California Youth Authority where he taught physical education.

An active tournament fighter, Marchini was consistently rated as one of the top three in the United States from 1968 through 1972. Between 1968-70, he was rated number one. In 1970, he was elected to the Black Belt Hall of Fame. A member of the U.S. karate team which competed in the first World Karate Championships in 1970, Marchini made four trips to Japan to train under Master M. Koide of the Renbukai Karate Association. He presently holds a third degree black belt in rembukai karate and a third degree brown belt in judo.

Marchini presently devotes full time to various enterprises, including his partnership with Leo Fong in the Marchini-Fong Karate Schools in central California.

LEO T. FONG

Leo T. Fong was born in Canton, China in 1928, and immigrated to the United States with his parents when he was five years old. Athletics have been an integral part of his life since junior high school where he participated in football, track and boxing.

Fong is a graduate of Hendrix College in Conway, Arkansas where he received a Bachelor's degree in physical education, Southern Methodist University in Dallas, Texas where he obtained a Bachelor's degree in Theology, and California State University in Sacramento where he earned a Master's degree in social work.

Since meeting renowned physique star Bill Pearl, Fong has incorporated weight training as an important part of his exercising program. He has practiced kung-fu, tae kwon do and various forms of defensive arts since 1958. The martial artist is the author of two best selling kung-fu books, *Sil Lum Kung-Fu* and *Choy Lay Fut Kung-Fu.*

Mr. Fong has long known that his interest in the various forms of self-defense is boundless. Starting during his Hendrix College days, he began training with gloves and soon discovered that it was to provide more than just an energy-charged diversion from his curriculum of studies. The immediate fruits of this dedication was the collegiate boxing crown between 1949 and 1951. In addition, he fought his way into the Arkansas AAU finals in 1950 and into the finals of the Southwestern Golden Gloves in 1953.

Presently, he is applying his twelve years of practical experience in kung-fu to students of all ages who attend the Marchini-Fong Karate Schools of central California.

CONTENTS

TIPS FOR USING THIS BOOK

No person is a perfect fighting machine. Some fighters are fast but weak, others strong but slow, and still others are fast and strong, but lack stamina. The programs of exercises in the following chapters are designed to strengthen weak areas.

The greatest benefit can be derived through following these programs of exercises systematically and consistently. It is the authors' experience that a program of weight training combined with stretching, non-weight resistent exercises and good nutrition can produce the greatest results. (When the authors use the word, "consistently," they mean about three to four times a week.)

Each exercise in the book has a specific name. Some of the names are common and others not so common. In order to avoid confusion, the first chapter deals with programs of exercises to obtain specific desired results. These exercises are illustrated in subsequent chapters with their application to a specific karate technique.

In order to acquaint yourself with the exercises in the book, it is advisable to read the whole book through several times to get an overall view of its content and decide which program you wish to follow at the outset.

GENERAL TRAINING HINTS

1. Warm up properly.
2. Wear warm clothing.
3. Have good ventilation.
4. Always train with a partner.
5. Clear your mind of disrupting thoughts.
6. Get plenty of sleep.
7. Eat nutritious food.
8. Use quality food supplements.
9. Keep warm between sets.
10. Keep a regular training schedule.
11. Don't cheat on exercises—do them as strictly as possible.
12. Remember, there is no set weight for all exercises. Use your good judgment.
13. Expect to be sore after the first few workouts.
14. Don't expect miracles. Progress takes time and patience.

NOTE: For the benefit of the beginner, laymen's terms are used in most cases to describe the various muscles in the glossary of exercises. Instead of using words such as deltoids, the authors substitute "the shoulder muscles"; pectoralis, "chest muscles", etcetera.

GLOSSARY of WEIGHT LIFTING EXERCISES

EXERCISE	MUSCLES DEVELOPED	
1. Abdominal leg pulls on extension machine	Lower abdominal muscles	
2. Back fist punch exercise with hand weights	Pectorals and triceps	
3. Back stance barbell exercise	Thighs and calves	
4. Barbell bicep curls	Biceps and forearms	
5. Barbell curl and press	Triceps and shoulders	
6. Barbell neck bridge	Neck and chest	
7. Barbell sliding side horse exercise	Legs and trunk	
8. Bench press	Chest, shoulders and triceps	
9. Bent arm laterals	Chest, shoulders and triceps	
10. Bent over laterals	Upper back and shoulders	
11. Bent over rowing	Back and triceps	
12. Bomb 21 tricep curls	Triceps	
13. Calf heel raises	Calves and back	
14. Circular dumbbell blocking exercise	Shoulders, arms and forearms	
15. Dumbbell calf raises	Calves and feet	
16. Dumbbell pullovers	Front shoulder and upper lat muscles	
17. Dumbbell wrist curls	Wrists, forearms and fingers	
18. Front neck curls	Neck	
19. Front stance barbell exercise	Thighs and calves	
20. Front squat	Knees and thighs	
21. Full squats	Thighs	
22. Hack squats	Knees and thighs	
23. Half squats	Thighs and lower trunk	
24. Inward blocking exercise with hand weights	Arms, forearms and shoulders	
25. Lat pull downs	Shoulders and neck	
26. Leg curls on extension machine	Back of thighs and calves	
27. Leg extensions on machine	Thigh and knee muscles	

TECHNIQUES ENHANCED

Kicking

All outward blocking motions

Back stance

Grabbing and hooking motions

Punching, thrusting and chopping

Blow absorption

Mobility in the horse stance

Punching and striking

Elbow strikes, reverse punches and the U-punch

Backhand striking and blocking motions

Pulling and grabbing motions

Forward punching

Kicking and thrusting motions

Circular blocking and punching motions

Kicking and thrusting motions and pushing-off power

Pulling and grappling motions

Grabbing, finger striking and pinching motions

Blow absorption

Punching, blocking and striking

All kicking (especially the front kick) and thrusting motions

All kicking and thrusting motions

All kicking and thrusting motions

Kicking, thrusting and stance solidification

Inward blocking and striking motions

Grappling and hooking motions

All hooking and kickback motions

Front kicking and snapping motions

CONTINUED

EXERCISE	MUSCLES DEVELOPED	
28. Leg raises	Lower abdominal muscles	
29. Lower trunk extensions	Lower abdominal muscles and upper thighs	
30. Lunge punch exercise with hand weights	Wrists and shoulders	
31. Neck with headstrap	Neck	
32. One arm dumbbell rowing	Back and arm muscles	
33. Open hand blocking exercise with hand weights	Wrists, forearms and shoulders	
34. Outward blocking exercise with hand weights	Wrists, forearms and shoulders	
35. Pinch grip circular barbell plate	Wrists, fingers and forearms	
36. Push-up with weight	Chest, shoulders and backs of arms	
37. Reverse dips on bench	Forearms, triceps and shoulders	
38. Reverse punch exercise with hand weights	Forearms and shoulders	
39. Reverse wrist curls	Forearms and wrists	
40. Rising block with hand weights	Shoulders and arms	
41. Seated alternate dumbbell presses	Shoulders, back or arms and upper back	
42. Seated barbell curls	Lower biceps and forearms	
43. Seated barbell french curls	Back, shoulders and lats	
44. Seated calf raises	Ankles and calves	
45. Seated dumbbell curls	Biceps and forearms	
46. Sit-ups on bench	Upper abdominal muscles	
47. Sit-ups on incline board	Abdominal muscles	
48. Square horse exercise	Thighs and trunk	
49. Standing laterals	Shoulders and upper back	
50. Standing press	Shoulders and upper back	
51. Tricep extension on lat machine	Triceps	
52. Tricep pushdown on lat machine	Triceps and shoulders	
53. Twist horse barbell exercise	Thighs and calves	
54. Upright rowing	Shoulders	

TECHNIQUES ENHANCED

Hip-snapping actions for front kicking

Snapping motions in the delivery of thrusts and strikes

Penetration power of lunge punch

All motions which use the head as a weapon

Pulling and tugging movements for sweeps and throws

Open hand blocking and chopping strikes

Blocking and striking against strong body punches

Grabbing and clawing actions

Punching and chopping

Punching and blocking

Penetration power of reverse punch

Punching and grabbing motions

Rising block against overhead attacks

Punching, striking and blocking

Grabbing and hooking motions

Outward and downward blocking motions

Kicking and sweeping motions

Grabbing and hooking motions

Bodily snap for punching and striking

Punching and thrusting motions which require hip action

Horse stance and kicking from this stance

Outward blocking and backhand striking motions

Power punching, eye stabbing, blocking, thrusting and pushing

Outward and downward blocking and chopping motions

Outward and downward blocking and chopping motions

Kicking and shifting mobility in horse stance

Sweeps and throws

WEIGHT LIFTING EXERCISES

BENCH PRESS

(1) Begin with your arms fully extended, holding the weight with your back straight along the bench and your feet flat on the floor. (2) Let the bar down gradually, exhaling and keeping it even as it is lowered to your chest. (3 & 4) After the bar touches the tip of your pectoral

muscles, pause slightly to push up, being sure not to arch your back. (5) Extend the bar arm's length and repeat the cycle.

The bench press will benefit the chest, shoulder and tricep muscles, enhancing all of your punching and striking movements.

DUMBBELL CROSSOVERS

(1) Lying back squarely on the bench, extend your arms upward and hold the dumbbells end to end. (2) Inhale, and cross your arms right over left as far as they will go. (3) Exhale when the dumbbells are fully lowered. (4-6) Lift the dumbbells slowly back until your arms are extended outward, being sure to use only the

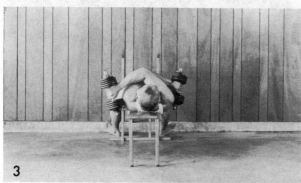

strength of your arms. (7 & 8) Raise your arms to cross over above you and repeat this process, alternating right over left and left over right.

These dumbbell crossovers develop the muscles in your chest and in the front of your shoulders, increasing power in all backfist and back elbow strikes.

1

BENT ARM LATERALS

(1) With your arms extended and the dumbbells together, be sure to keep your back straight and your feet on the floor. (2) Inhale slowly as you begin to lower the dumbbells until, (3) they are even with your chest. (4 & 5) Exhale as you raise the dumbbells

2

up to the original extended arms position again and repeat the cycle.

The bent arm laterals develop the chest, shoulders and the backs of your arms, increasing your power for elbow strikes, reverse punches and the "U" punch.

1

2

DUMBBELL PULLOVERS

(1) Begin with your back straight along the bench and your feet flat on the floor. Grip the weight with both hands, palms upward. Be sure your arms are straight and your head is slightly upward. (2) Inhale and lower the dumbbell behind your neck until (3) you have lowered it as far as possible. Remem-

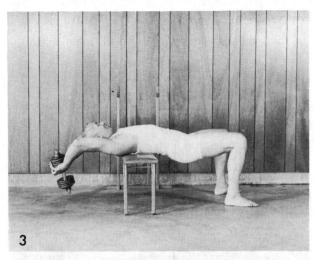

3

ber to keep your arms straight at all times. (4 & 5) Slowly return the weight to its starting position, exhaling as you go.

This exercise will develop the front part of your shoulders and the upper lat muscles under your arms which will enhance your pulling and grappling motions.

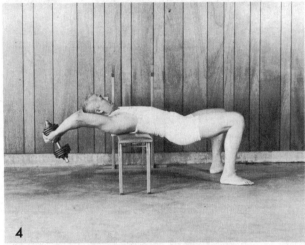

4

5

PUSH UP
WITH WEIGHT

(1) Assume the prone position, supporting your weight on the knuckles of both hands with your back straight. Have someone place a weight on the middle of your back. (2) Then lower your body, inhaling as you go, remembering to keep your back and legs straight at all times. (3-5) Touch

the floor with your chest and exhale as you slowly push yourself up into the starting position.

Doing push-ups with a weight develops the chest, shoulders and the backs of the arms for increased power in your punching and chopping motions.

STANDING PRESS

(1) With your knees bent and your feet flat on the floor, look straight ahead and get a medium grip on the bar. (2) Bring the weight up to your chest level and exhale when this is done. Be sure your legs are doing the work in this maneuver. (3 & 4) Inhale, and press the weight to arms length and then exhale. (5 & 6)

Lower the weight back to your chest and repeat the press. When you finish the exercise, be sure to bend your legs and not your back in returning the weight to the floor.

This standing press develops the shoulder and upper back muscles for power punching, eye stabbing, blocking, thrusting and pushing.

UPRIGHT ROWING

(1) Standing erect, grip the bar with your hands close together and (2) inhale while you pull the bar to your upper chest. (3 & 4) Exhale and lower the bar to the starting position before repeating the cycle.

Upright rowing develops your shoulder muscles, strengthening your blocking motions and your lifting actions for sweeps and throws.

1

2

SEATED ALTERNATE DUMBBELL PRESSES

(1) From the sitting position, put the dumbbells on your shoulders while keeping your back straight. (2) Inhale and press the right dumbbell up. (3) Return it. (4) Raise the left one, and (5) repeat the cycle over and over.

The seated dumbbell presses develop the backs of your arms, your shoulders and upper back muscles and strengthen your punching, striking and blocking motions.

STANDING LATERALS

(1) Stand erect with the dumbbells at your side, and look straight ahead. (2 & 3) Inhale and bring the weights up to your shoulder level, keeping your arms straight. (3) Pause and exhale as you lower the dumbbells and (5) return to the starting

position before repeating the movements.

The standing laterals develop muscles in the shoulders and upper back, strengthening your outward blocking and backhand striking motions.

BENT OVER LATERALS

(1) With your knees slightly bent, begin holding the weights in a crouched-over position. (2 & 3) Inhale as you bring the weights to shoulder level. (4 & 5) Pause slightly and slowly lower the weights while you exhale, being

sure to return to the
starting position before
repeating the cycle.

Bent over laterals devel-
op your upper back and
shoulder muscles, facili-
tating all backhand
striking and blocking
motions.

BENT OVER ROWING

(1) With your knees slightly bent, bend over and get a medium grip on the bar. (2) Inhale, and pull the bar upwards (3) until it reaches the chest. (4 & 5) Keeping your body bent, exhale while you lower the bar

slowly back into starting position before repeating the process.

Bent over rowing develops the back muscles and helps you in your pulling and grappling motions.

ONE ARM DUMBBELL ROWINGS

(1) With your left hand on a bench and your knees slightly bent, grasp the weight in your right hand. (2) Inhale, and pull the weight upwards until (3) it reaches chest level. (4) Remaining bent over, exhale as you lower the dumbbell to its starting

40

position. Repeat the process with slow and deliberate motions.

One arm dumbbell rowings help your back and arm muscles and strengthen all pulling and tugging movements for sweeps and throws.

LAT PULL DOWNS

(1) Keeping your back straight, get a wide grip on the lat bar. (2) Inhale and pull the bar slowly as far down as possible until (3) it reaches the back of your neck. (4 & 5) Exhale while you let the bar slowly pull your arms upward (6) until they are extended and ready to start the process over again.

These lat pull-downs will eventually help your grappling and hooking motions.

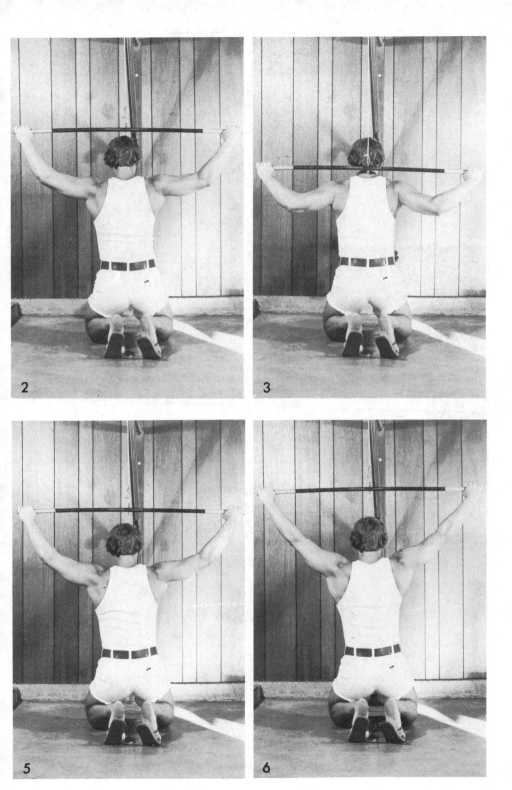

TRICEP PUSHDOWN ON LAT MACHINE

(1) Leaning back against the bar, get a close grip with your hands, while making sure to keep your back and legs straight. (2) Using the strength in only your arms, push the bar down while inhaling. (3) Exhale as you allow the bar to slowly return.

The tricep pushdown is useful in bolstering your outward and downward motions and your chopping.

TRICEP EXTENSIONS ON LAT MACHINE

(1) Get a close grip on the bar, keeping your elbows tight into your body, your legs straight and your shoulders down. (2) Exhale as you push the bar steadily downward. Be sure to concentrate the pressure in the backs of your arms without any jerking motions. (3) After your arms are extended downward, (4 & 5) inhale while the bar slowly returns to its original position. (6) Return to starting position and begin the cycle again.

This exercise develops the triceps and strengthens your chopping, and outward and downward blocking motions.

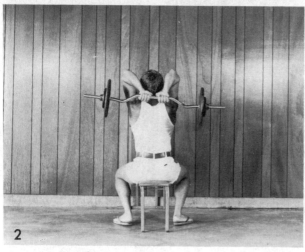

SEATED BARBELL FRENCH CURLS

(1) With your hands gripping the bar close together, and your arms extended overhead, begin with a straight back and both feet on the floor. Keeping the elbows as close to the head as possible, (2) lower the bar behind

your head as far as possible. (3, 4 & 5) Exhale as the bar is slowly returned to the starting position.

This exercise will help you in your outward and downward blocking motions.

BARBELL CURL
AND PRESS

(1) With your back flat on the bench, extend your arms overhead with a medium grip on the barbell. (2 & 3) Curl the bar behind your neck, pausing to exhale and lower the bar as much as possible. (4) From behind the neck position, pull the bar over your head and bring it down slowly on your chest, inhaling s i m u l t aneously. (5)

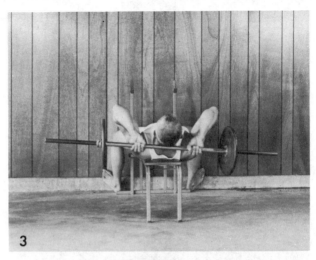

From the chest position, raise your arms to their starting position and exhale before repeating the process.

This barbell curl and press strengthens your punching, thrusting and chopping abilities in addition to outward and downward blocking motions.

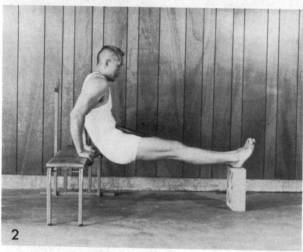

REVERSE DIPS
ON THE BENCH

(1) With your arms extending straight downward behind you, and your body and legs rigid, have a partner place a barbell plate on your lower abdomen. (2 & 3) Inhale and lower your body slowly until it comes to rest near your

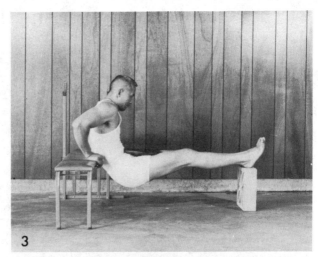

hands. (4 & 5) Exhale while you use the muscles in the backs of your arms to push yourself into the original position.

The exercise strengthens blocking and punching motions.

BOMB 21 TRICEP CURLS

(1) With your feet flat on the floor and your back flat on the bench, extend your arms with a close grip on the bar. (2) Lower the bar slowly and inhale until you are midway to your head. (3) Return to starting position and repeat the process 7 times. (4 & 5) From the midway position, lower the bar to your head after inhaling. (6) Return the bar to the midway position and repeat this 7 times. (7) With your arms extended in the original starting position, do a full tricep curl and (8) repeat the process 7 times, inhaling as the bar is lowered and (9) exhaling as your arms are extended.

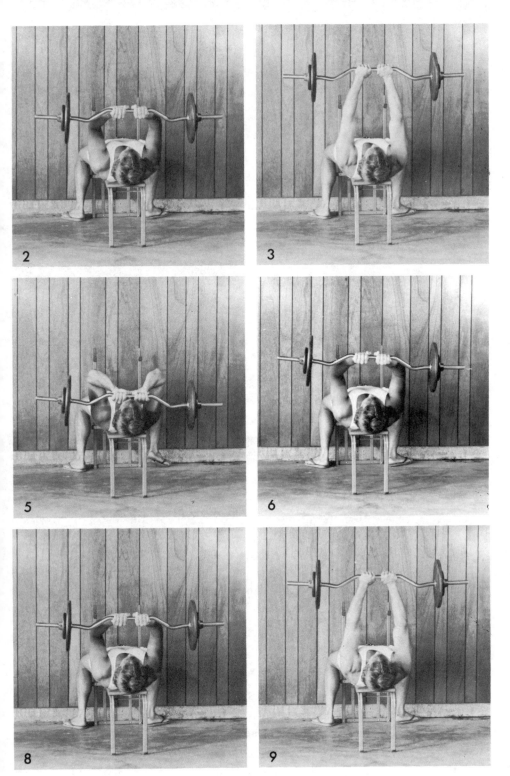

BARBELL BICEP CURLS

(1) Standing with your back and legs straight, apply a medium grip on the barbell. (2) Inhale and curl the barbell with the biceps. Do not throw your hip into movements, but keep as rigid as possible. (3) In this manner, raise the barbell slowly to your chin. (4 & 5) Exhale as the weight is slowly lowered into starting position.

This exercise will strengthen all of your grabbing and hooking motions.

SEATED DUMBBELL CURLS

(1) Looking straight ahead, with your back rigid, hold the dumbbells at your side. (2) Turn your palms upward, inhale, and begin curling the dumbbells until (3) they are even with your shoulders. Remember to concentrate this action in your biceps. (4) Exhale as the dumbbells are returned to their starting position.

Your grabbing and hooking motions will be enhanced by this exercise.

SEATED BARBELL CURLS

(1) With your body erect, your feet flat on the floor and looking straight ahead, begin with the barbell on the thighs. (2) Inhale as you curl the barbell upwards to the neck, and (3) exhale as the barbell is lowered slowly to its starting position. Be sure you do not cheat by swinging your body to do the work your biceps are supposed to be doing.

If performed correctly, this exercise will strengthen the lower bicep and forearms for grabbing and hooking motions.

FULL SQUATS

(1) With your feet positioned at shoulder width and your back straight, begin with the bar on your shoulders. (2) Inhale and begin to squat slowly until (3) your buttocks touch your calves. Be sure you are not bouncing in this exercise. (4 & 5) Keeping

your back straight and your chest out, exhale as the squat is brought back to the starting position.

This is beneficial to your thighs and will help you in all kicking and other thrusting motions of the legs.

HACK SQUATS

(1) With your back straight, your arms extended and your hands spaced a bit wider than shoulder width, grasp the bar with your palms facing to the rear and keep your buttocks on the bar. (2) Inhale and stand up slowly, being sure to keep the bar against your buttocks

until (3) you are standing erect. (4) Exhale as you squat slowly with the bar to its original starting position. (5) Remember to keep your body rigid at all times while bending only your knees.

This exercise is beneficial to all kicking and leg thrusting.

HALF SQUATS

(1) Begin standing with your back straight and the bar resting on the front of your shoulders. (2) Inhale and squat slowly until you reach the halfway point, at which time you exhale and complete the squat. (3) Return to the starting position, remembering to keep your back straight.

The half squat develops the lower trunk and will strengthen your kicking and thrusting motions as well as solidifying your karate stances.

FRONT SQUAT

(1) Begin in the squat position, looking straight ahead with a medium grip on the bar. (2) From the squat position, clean the bar to your chest while you inhale, being sure your palms are faced upward. (3) Supporting the weight on your chest and arms, stand erect and exhale. (4) Return to the squat position and repeat the exercise, always inhaling on the squat and exhaling on completion of the squat. Remember that this is a leg exercise and that you should not be bouncing.

The front squat will develop your knee and thigh muscles, which strengthen all kicking and thrusting motions, particularly the front kick.

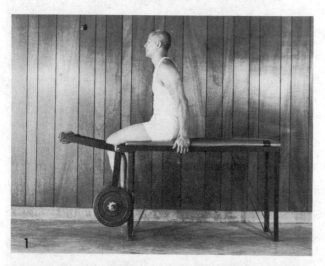

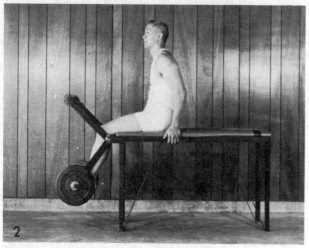

LEG EXTENSIONS ON MACHINE

(1) Sitting on the bench with your body as straight as possible, begin with your legs behind the extension bar, making sure it comes across the insteps of your feet. (2) While you inhale, extend your legs straight out, (3) remembering to keep your

body straight. Pause before you lower the bar (4 & 5) and exhale at the completion of the movement.

Leg extensions help the thigh and knee muscles and will strengthen your front kicking and snapping motions.

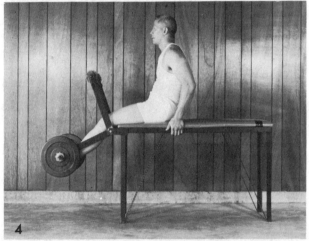

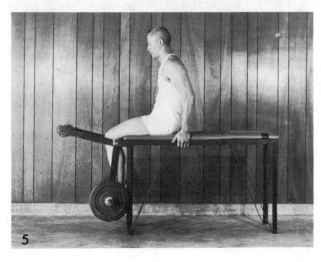

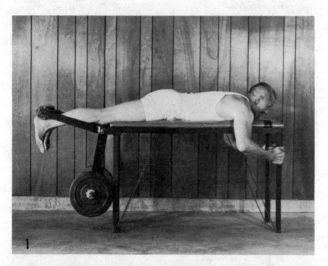

LEG CURLS ON EXTENSION MACHINE

(1) Lying face down on the extension machine, hook both of your heels beneath the bar. (2) Remembering to keep your buttock down, inhale and curl the weights back toward your buttocks with your legs. (3) Curl the bar back as far as possible, (4 & 5) and

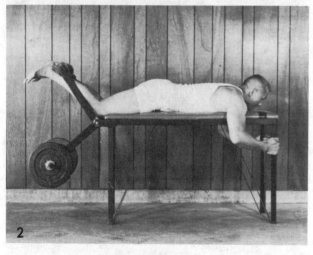

be sure to pause before lowering the weights back into starting position. Remember to exhale while lowering the bar.

This exercise will develop the back parts of your legs and aid you in all hooking and kick back motions.

NECK WITH HEAD STRAP

(1) Keeping your back straight, your legs slightly bent and your hands on your knees, (2) inhale and lift the weight up with your neck only. (3) Lift your neck without leaving the stance and (4) exhale as you lower your neck back into starting posi-

tion. Be sure that the weight never touches the floor.

Your neck muscles will benefit from this exercise, and will facilitate movements which use the head as a weapon.

FRONT NECK CURLS

(1) Keeping your back flat along the bench and your feet on the floor, hold the dumbbell to your forehead with a towel in-between for a cushion. (2 & 3) Inhale and curl your head toward your chest, being sure that your hands do not aid the movements of your neck. (4) Exhale as you lower your head to (5) the starting position.

Front neck curls will develop the defensive prowess of your neck, protecting it against blows.

BARBELL NECK BRIDGE

(1) Cushioning your head against the floor, hold the barbell on your chest with a medium grip. (2) Exhale, bridge on your neck and push the barbell to the arms extended position. (3) Lower the barbell to its starting position, remembering to maintain a bridged position.

This exercise develops the neck and chest muscles, strengthening your ability to absorb blows in these areas.

REVERSE WRIST CURLS

(1) With both arms resting on your knees, grip the dumbbell with your palm downward, allowing your wrist to hang slightly over your knee. (2 & 3) Curl the dumbbell upwards as far as it will go. (4 & 5) Pause

slightly before lowering the dumbbell slowly to its starting position.

Your forearms will be helped most by this exercise, allowing you to strengthen your punching and grabbing motions.

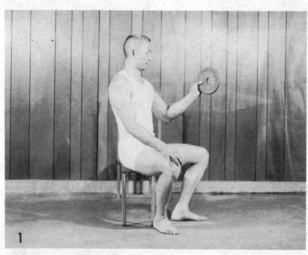

PINCH GRIP CIRCULAR BARBELL PLATE

(1) Begin by sitting straight in a bench and grip a ten pound barbell plate between your thumb and fingers. Be sure to keep your elbow at least three inches from your chest. (2-5) Using only the muscles of your wrist, make circular motions with the

plate, going clockwise
first and then counter-
clockwise. Be sure to
perform these motions
slowly for maximum
effect.

This will develop your
wrists, fingers and fore-
arms to help you in your
grabbing and clawing
actions.

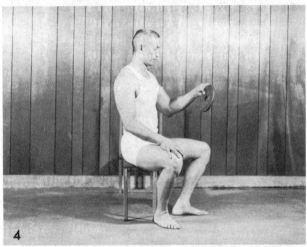

DUMBBELL WRIST CURLS

(1) Begin by resting your forearm on one knee, and grip the dumbbell in your hand, palm upwards. (2-4) Using the strength of your wrist, curl the dumbbell toward you and then lower it by letting it roll all the way to your fingertips. Repeat this action, being sure to do it slowly.

The wrist curl will strengthen your wrists, forearms and fingers, enhancing all of your grabbing, finger striking and pinching motions.

LEG RAISES

(1) Begin with your body flat along the incline board, grasping the strap at the raised end. (2) Inhale and lift your legs until they are perpendicular with the floor. (3) Exhale as you slowly lower your legs back into the starting position.

These leg raises will develop your lower abdominal muscles and strengthen all kicking and striking motions by improving your hip snapping actions.

CALF HEEL RAISES

(1) Begin with the barbell squarely on your shoulders, your body erect and your feet pointed outward at about shoulder width. (2) Inhale and raise yourself as far as you can on your toes. (3) Pause and then exhale as you return to the starting position. (4) Now turn your feet inwards slightly so that the toes are pointed straight ahead. (5) Inhale and raise yourself up on your toes as far as possible. (6) Pause and then lower yourself until your feet are again flat on the ground. (7) Now move your feet again until the toes are pointed in slightly. (8) Raise up on your toes, inhaling as you go up, and (9) exhaling as you come down with your feet flat on the floor.

The calf heel raises will ultimately strengthen your kicking and thrusting motions.

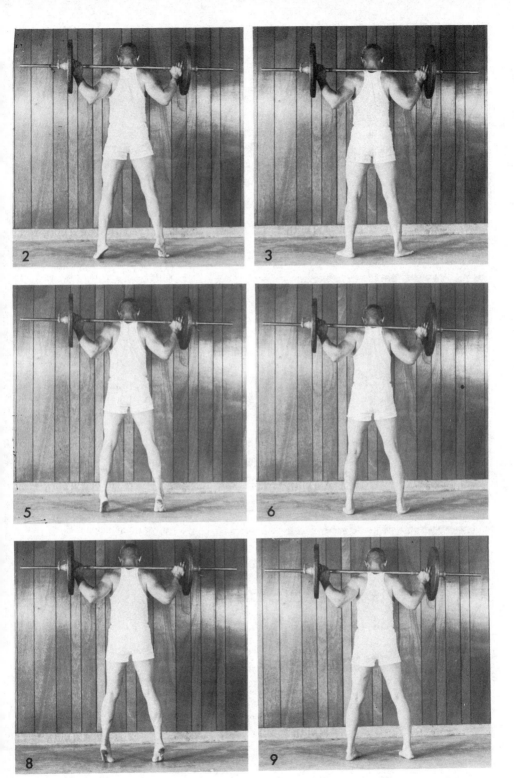

DUMBBELL CALF RAISES

(1) Begin by standing with your left foot on a block and your right leg raised. Hold the dumbbell in your left hand. (2) Inhale and raise up on your left foot as far as you can go. (3) Pause slightly and exhale while you return to the starting position. After you repeat this the desired number of times, exercise using the other foot.

This exercise will develop your calves and your foot muscles which serve to strengthen kicking and thrusting motions of the legs as well as pushing off power on attacks.

SEATED
CALF RAISES

(1) Sitting erect on a bench, place the barbell on your knees while your feet are flat on the floor and spread about shoulder width. (2) Inhale and push upward with your toes. (3) Exhale and return to the starting position.

This exercise will strengthen all of your kicking and sweeping motions.

SIT UPS ON INCLINE BOARD

(1) Begin by hooking your feet beneath the strap on the incline board. Keep your legs slightly bent and your hands locked behind your head. (2) Exhale and sit up slowly until (3) your head meets your knees. Inhale as you lower your trunk slowly to begin the cycle again.

This exercise benefits your abdominal muscles and strengthens your thrusting and punching motions which require hip action.

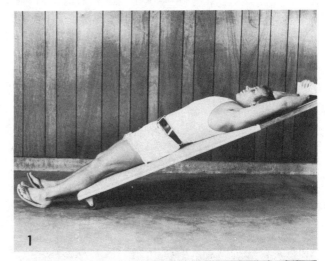

LOWER TRUNK EXTENSION

(1) Begin by gripping the strap at the higher end of the incline board. Be sure to lie flat along the board. (2) Exhale and raise your legs slowly until (3) they are parallel with the board. Inhale as you lower your legs slowly into the starting position, being sure to keep the tension on your lower abdominal muscles.

The lower trunk extension will be useful to you for your snapping motions in the delivery of thrusts and strikes.

SIT UPS ON BENCH

(1) Begin by sitting straight up on the bench, anchoring your feet under a fairly heavy barbell. Be sure to hold an empty bar against the back of your neck with about a shoulder-and-a-half width grip. (2) Inhale and slowly lower your body until (3) you touch the floor with the

backs of your shoulders. (4 & 5) Pause slightly and exhale as you slowly sit up again to the starting position.

This exercise will develop your upper abdominal muscles for punching and striking motions that require the snapping of the body.

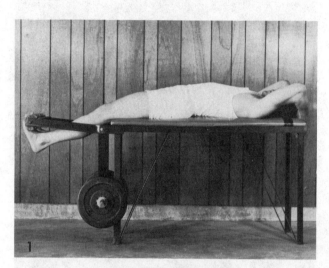

ABDOMINAL LEG PULLS ON EXTENSION MACHINE

(1) Lie flat along the extension machine, grasping the end of the bench with both hands and hooking your feet beneath the extension bar. (2) Inhale and bring your knees toward your chest until (3) they are almost perpendicular to the ground. Be sure you

are keeping the tension on your abdominal muscles. (4 & 5) Exhale as you lower your feet slowly back into starting position.

This exercise will strengthen your lower abdominal muscles, helping your kicking motions.

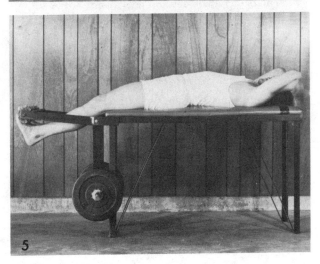

SQUARE HORSE EXERCISE

(1) Begin by placing the barbell on your shoulders and behind your head. Remembering to keep your back straight, and to look straight ahead, assume a half squat position with your feet slightly wider apart than shoulder width. (2) Pivot clockwise on your left foot, being sure to maintain your original posture and maneuvering your body until (3) you are in a side horse. (4) From this side horse position, pivot now on your right foot in a clockwise direction. (5) Pivot once again on the left foot clockwise until (6) you are in another side horse position. (7 & 8) Pivot on your right foot in a clockwise direction until you finally assume the original starting position.

This exercise will develop your thighs and trunk which serve to strengthen your horse stance and your kicking.

CIRCULAR DUMBBELL
BLOCKING EXERCISE

(1) Begin the exercise holding the dumbbells, your left arm extended and your right arm bent. (2) Execute circular motions with the dumbbells in a clockwise direction for your left hand and a counterclockwise direction for your right. (3) Alternate this exercise, first to your left and then to your right.

Your shoulder, arm and forearm muscles will benefit from this exercise, which will help your circular block and punching motions.

BARBELL SLIDING
SIDE HORSE EXERCISE

(1) Begin in a regular horse stance, holding the barbell along the back of your shoulders with a wide grip. (2) Making sure to keep your back straight, slide to the left by leading off with your left foot and following with your right foot. (3 & 4) In sliding to the right, lead off with your right foot and follow with your left. You should slide the length of the room in this way before reversing your direction.

This exercise will strengthen your legs and trunk and will develop mobility in your horse stance.

FRONT STANCE
BARBELL EXERCISE

(1) Begin by holding the barbell on your shoulders and behind your neck. Be sure your left leg is bent in front of you with about sixty percent of your weight resting on it. (2) Keeping your body straight and looking straight ahead, shift your stance by sliding the right leg forward and (3) your left leg back. Remember

to keep most of your weight on the front leg at all times. (4 & 5) Shift again to the original starting position by sliding your right leg back and your left leg forward.

This exercise will strengthen your front stance for more powerful punching, blocking and striking motions.

BACK STANCE
BARBELL EXERCISE

(1) Keeping your body straight, begin the exercise with the barbell along your shoulders and behind your neck. (2) Slide your left foot forward along the floor, placing about sixty percent of your weight on your back leg. This is the left leg back stance. (3 & 4)

From here, shift into a right leg back stance by sliding your right foot forward and shifting your weight to your left foot, which is now your back foot.

This exercise will strengthen your back stance for kicking, punching, blocking and striking.

TWIST HORSE
BARBELL EXERCISE

(1) Keeping your body erect and looking straight ahead, begin with the barbell on your shoulders and behind your neck. (2) Slide your left foot slightly forward and twist it outward. (3) Now twist your body to the left until your right leg is braced against the back of your left knee. Hold this position for a ten count. (4) From this twist horse

stance, shift your right leg slowly, until (5) you are in a regular horse stance. (6 & 7) Repeating the motions you used when leading with your left foot, twist until you are once again in a regular front horse stance (8).

This exercise will strengthen your kicking and shifting.

1

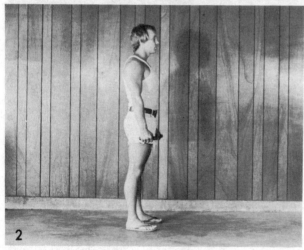

2

REVERSE PUNCH EXERCISE WITH HAND WEIGHTS

(1) Begin by holding t h r e e - pound hand-weights in a standing position with (2) your hands at your sides. (3) Move into a cover stance by sliding your right leg back, cocking your right arm and blocking with your left arm. (4 & 5) From this stance, exe-

cute a reverse punch, over and over. Repeat this process from the opposite stance when your required number of repetitions is completed.

The reverse punch exercise will develop your shoulder and arm muscles.

LUNGE PUNCH EXERCISE WITH HAND WEIGHTS

(1) Begin by assuming a cover stance with your body straight and holding the three-pound handweights, one in each hand. Be sure that about sixty percent of your weight rests on your front leg. (2) Slide your right foot forward along the ground and punch with your right hand. Repeat this for the necessary number of repetitions.

This exercise will help the penetration power of your lunge punch.

BACK FIST PUNCH EXERCISE WITH HAND WEIGHTS

(1) Begin in a horse stance, gripping one three-pound handweight in each hand. Keep your body erect, your weight evenly distributed and your feet spaced slightly past shoulder width. (2) Cross your left arm over your right arm and (3 & 4) strike out with a back fist. Remember to turn your head toward the direction of the punch. After you complete the repetitions, reverse your stance and begin striking with your right hand.

This exercise will strengthen your back fist blocking motion as well as all other outward blocking motions.

OPEN HAND BLOCKING EXERCISES WITH HAND WEIGHTS

(1) Begin in a back stance with sixty percent of your weight on your back leg. Be sure to hold the weights tucked between the palm of your hand and your thumb. Your right hand should be about mid-chest high with the palm facing upward. (2) Slide your right foot forward and shift into a right open hand block by crossing your right arm over your left. (3) Strike out with your right hand.

This exercise will strengthen your open hand blocking motions and your chopping strikes.

RISING BLOCK
WITH HAND
WEIGHTS

(1) Begin from a cover stance, with sixty percent of your weight on your front leg, your body straight and your eyes straight ahead. (2) Slide your right foot forward and bring your right hand to your chest. (3) Shift into a rising block by blocking upward with your right arm and bringing your left fist to the side of your rib cage. Repeat this process with your left side.

This exercise develops your shoulder and arm muscles, enhancing your rising block for parrying all overhead attacks.

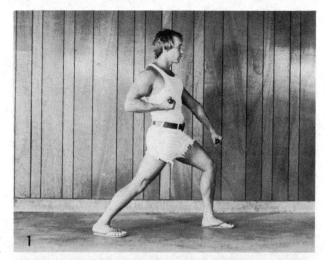

OUTWARD BLOCKING EXERCISE WITH HAND WEIGHTS

(1) Begin in the cover stance. (2) Begin to shift your right leg forward, cross your right arm under your left and hold the weight with the palm downward. (3) Block outward with your right arm while you are still sliding your right leg forward. Your fist should be in line with your shoulder. Repeat this process on the left side.

This exercise will develop your arm, forearm and shoulder muscles, enhancing your blocking and striking motions against strong body punches.

INWARD BLOCKING EXERCISE WITH HAND WEIGHTS

(1) Begin in a cover stance with your body straight and your eyes looking straight ahead. (2) As you hold the weights, shift your right leg forward and bring your right hand over your shoulder. (3) With a twisting motion of your right hand, execute an inward block. Repeat this process with your left hand.

This exercise will develop your arm, forearm and shoulder muscles for inward blocking and striking motions.

WEIGHT ROUTINES

The following pages deal with actual training programs used by the authors in developing power for karate and kung-fu. The exercises are divided into programs to obtain specific results. In addition to a program for beginners, there are also programs for those who would like to develop bulk and strength, speed and

BEGINNER'S WEIGHT ROUTINE

Use medium weights that can be handled comfortably. Train three days a week.

EXERCISES

Bench Press	3 sets	8 repetitions	(see page 18)
Dead Lifts	3 sets	8 repetitions	(not shown)
Squats	3 sets	8 repetitions	(see page 58)
Standing Press	3 sets	8 repetitions	(see page 28)
Barbell Curls	3 sets	8 repetitions	(see page 46)

GENERAL HINTS FOR BEGINNER'S ROUTINE

The purpose of the beginners program is to aid those who are interested in developing overall basic physical conditioning. This is an introductory routine to benefit those who have never utilized weight training. To derive the best results from this routine, the following training tips are important:

1. Use medium weights with medium repetitions of the exercises (approximately eight to 10 repetitions per set).
2. Train with weights three days per week on a regular basis. Remember, shoddy workouts produce shoddy results.
3. Perform each exercise as strictly as possible without unnecessary cheating movements.
4. Use a poundage that will allow you to complete all sets and repetitions of the exercises.
5. Keep the body warm at all times. Do not allow muscles to cool off.
6. Allow yourself approximately 30 seconds of rest between sets.
7. As a novice, do not try to perform an excessive amount of exercise. Work up gradually as progress is being made.
8. After the initial workout, muscle soreness will result for a few days.

endurance, advanced split routines, and a program of resistant exercises that can be performed without weights or supplemented by weight training. The complete programs on these pages are designed not only to develop strength, but also speed and endurance.

DEFINITION AND
ENDURANCE WEIGHT ROUTINE

1. Bench Press   5 sets   15 repetitions (see page 18)
2. Standing Press   4 sets   15 repetitions (see page 28)
3. One-half Squats   4 sets   20 repetitions (see page 63)
4. Heel Raises   4 sets   25 repetitions (see page 78)
5. Dead Lifts   4 sets   10 repetitions (not shown)
6. Dumbbell Seated Curls   5 sets   30 repetitions (see page 76)
7. Bomb 21 Tricep Curls   5 sets   21 repetitions (see page 52)

Use light weights with minimum rest between sets for four days a week, every other day.

GENERAL HINTS FOR
DEFINITION AND
ENDURANCE ROUTINE

1. Use low weights and high repetitions.
2. Lift at a fast steady pace.
3. Exercise should cause increase in breathing.
4. Train four days a week.
5. Don't pause too long between exercises.
6. Rest between sets only as long as it takes to do the preceding set.
7. Keep warm at all times.
8. Take three deep breaths between sets.
9. Perform each exercise quickly but strictly.

This routine is recommended for those who wish to cut down on muscle size and to increase definition and endurance. It is an excellent routine for the overweight.

BULK AND STRENGTH WEIGHT ROUTINE

This program is designed for those who desire an increase in muscle size and greater strength. With a good food supplement, maximum gain in body weight can be attained.

1. Bench Press	1 set	10 repetitions	(see page 18)
	1 set	6 repetitions	
	1 set	4 repetitions	
	1 set	2 repetitions	
	1 set	1 repetition	
2. Standing Press	(Use same as above)		(see page 28)
3. Squats	(Use same as above)		(see page 58)
4. Dead Lifts	(Use same as above)		(not shown)
5. Barbell Curls	(Use same as above)		(see page 46)
6. Tricep Extensions	(Use same as above)		(see page 45)

It is important that weight be added with each set until the maximum is reached for one repetition. Train three days a week, with a day of rest in between.

NOTE: Be sure to allow yourself a brief period of rest between sets. Usually a three to four minute span will suffice. This period will allow your muscles to regain some of their strength for the next set.

GENERAL HINTS FOR
BULK AND STRENGTH ROUTINE

1. Heavy weights and low repetitions.
2. Increase poundage as repetitions decrease.
3. Use maximum poundage for each set.
4. Warm up properly before attempting heavy weights.
5. Warm up with 10 repetitions with a light weight to prepare the body for heavy lifting and to get the proper movements for the exercise.
6. Train three to four days per week.
7. Push and tax yourself on the last repetition for increased poundage.
8. Take three deep breaths between sets.
9. Slight cheating movements are allowed to achieve maximum poundage.
10. Rest 30 seconds between sets.

ADVANCED SPLIT WEIGHT ROUTINE

Exercises for the upper body—to be done on Monday, Wednesday and Friday

1. Bench Press	5 sets	8 repetitions	(see page	18)
2. Chest Crossovers	5 sets	10 repetitions	(see page	20)
3. Standing Press	5 sets	8 repetitions	(see page	28)
4. Lateral Raises	5 sets	6 repetitions	(see page	34)
5. Lat Pulldowns	5 sets	10 repetitions	(see page	42)
6. Barbell Curls	5 sets	6 repetitions	(see page	54)
7. Dumbbell Seated Curls	5 sets	10 repetitions	(see page	76)
8. Barbell French Curls	5 sets	8 repetitions	(see page	46)
9. Tricep Pushdowns	5 sets	10 repetitions	(see page	44)

Exercises for the lower body—to be done on Tuesday, Thursday and Saturday

1. Dead Lifts	5 sets	8 repetitions	(not shown)	
2. Squats	5 sets	8 repetitions	(see page	58)
3. Hack Squats	5 sets	8 repetitions	(see page	60)
4. Heel Raises	5 sets	15 repetitions	(see page	78)
5. Leg Extensions	5 sets	10 repetitions	(see page	64)
6. Leg Curls	5 sets	10 repetitions	(see page	66)
7. Sit Ups	5 sets	25 repetitions	(see page	82)
8. Front Squats	5 sets	6 repetitions	(see page	62)
9. Leg Raises	5 sets	25 repetitions	(see page	206)

The exercises in this program require fairly heavy poundage. *Before progressing to heavier weights, warm up with a light weight at the beginning of each exercise.*

GENERAL HINTS FOR
THE ADVANCED SPLIT WEIGHT ROUTINE

1. Practice six days a week.
2. Train the upper body on Monday, Wednesday and Friday.
3. Train the lower body on Tuesday, Thursday and Saturday.
4. This routine is designed only for those who are advanced in weight training.
5. This program can be adapted to either the bulk and strength or definition and endurance programs.
6. Get plenty of rest.
7. Train with weights in the morning and karate at night or vice-versa to get maximum results.
8. All heavy lifting must be done in conjunction with stretching exercises.

IRON HAND TRAINING EXERCISES

In the following chapter are some of the exercises used by kung-fu and karate practitioners for strengthening and hardening of the hands and for breaking bricks and boards. Kung-fu practitioners utilize these exercises to strengthen their fingers for the various clawing and jabbing techniques of self-defense found in most Chinese fighting systems.

BEAN BAG EXERCISE

(1) Begin by assuming the horse stance with the beanbag in your left hand. (2) From this position, toss the beanbag into the air and (3) grab it with your right hand. Be sure to dig your fingers into the bag as you catch it. Alternate this exercise using your left and right hands. (Note: When the bag becomes too light, fill it with B.B. shots. The bag in this particular illustration is filled with 15 pounds of buckshot.)

This exercise will develop your finger and forearm muscles, strengthening your clawing and grabbing motions.

CHOPPING EXERCISE ON SANDBAG

(1) Begin by assuming a low horse stance. Place a small sand or beanbag atop two basalite cement blocks. (2 & 3) Chop down on the bag with your right hand, being sure to give your hand a twist motion as you deliver the strike. Remember to relax your hand at the beginning when you approach the bag and tense it on contact. Repeat this exercise with each hand.

This drill will strengthen your chopping and blocking motions.

113

BACK FIST EXERCISE ON SANDBAG

(1) With the sandbag placed atop two basalite cement blocks, begin by assuming the horse stance. (2) Raise your right fist with the palm pointing outward. (3) Strike the sandbag with the back part of your fist, being sure to give your wrist a twisting motion as you make contact. Alternate this exercise using your right and left hands.

This will develop your forearm and the backs of your arms, enhancing all your back striking and outward blocking motions.

PUNCHING EXERCISE WITH SANDBAG

(1) Assume the horse stance and begin by cocking your right arm and making a fist. Keep your eyes on the sandbag, which is sitting on top of a single cement block. (2 & 3) Punch into the sandbag, letting your knuckles take the brunt of the blow, and remembering to make a twisting of the wrist on contact.

This exercise will develop your forearm, shoulder and arm muscles, strengthening all of your punching, thrusting and striking motions.

TIGER CLAWING EXERCISE ON RUBBER PAD

(1) Begin by assuming a comfortable kneeling position, with your right knee on the floor and your arm resting on the other leg. Be sure the rubber pad is placed squarely atop a single cement block. (2) Keeping your fingers and wrist limber, strike the rubber pad with a snapping motion. When your spread fingers

make contact with the pad, be sure to dig them in. (3 & 4) Retract your hand with a flick of the arm and repeat the process.

The tiger clawing exercise develops strong fingers and forearms to aid in all striking, clawing and jabbing techniques.

PRACTICAL APPLICATIONS OF KUNG-FU AND KARATE

This book is not a volume on the techniques of Karate and Kung-Fu, although this section will deal with some of the basic movements in the two arts. The primary focus of this section is to offer a cross reference of the basic and advanced exercises, with and without weights, that will add greater explosive power to your blocking, punching, striking, and thrusting movements, regardless of the system being practiced.

The techniques contained in this chapter are merely examples of how weight training exercises can supplement the improvement of these techniques.

The exercises mentioned in this chapter are explained in greater detail in the Exercise Glossary of this book. Reference to that section will aid in better comprehension of the specific exercises.

LUNGE PUNCH

(1 & 2) In **kung-fu,** begin in a left forward stance and slide your rear leg forward. (3) When your right foot becomes even with your left, slide your left foot back and initiate a right hand punch. (4) Lock your back leg out upon completion of the punch. (A) In karate, assume a left forward stance facing your opponent. (B) Step forward into a right forward stance (about 12 inches ahead of your original position) and execute a right hand punch to your opponent's jaw. **Supplementary weight exercises** include the Bench Press (see page 18), Bent Arm Laterals (see page 22), and Push Ups With Weight (see page 26).

FRONT PUNCH

(1-3) In **kung-fu**, begin in a left forward stance, put most of your weight on your front leg and execute a front punch. (4) Withdraw the punching hand and assume the original stance. (A & B) In **karate**, begin in a left forward stance and lean forward as you feint with your right hand. (C & D) Execute a

left front punch to your opponent's head and withdraw to the original stance. **Supplementary weight exercises** include the Bench Press (see page 18), Bent Arm Laterals (see page 22), and Push Ups With Weights (see page 26).

REVERSE PUNCH
(Kung-Fu)

(1) Assume a left forward stance. (2) From this position, slide your left foot forward and twist your hips with force to the left. Strike with your right hand while simultaneously withdrawing your left for added power. (3) Immediately after contact, withdraw your punch and assume the original left forward stance.

Supplementary weight exercises include:

1. Bench Press (see page 18)
2. Bent Arm Laterals (see page 22)
3. Push Ups With Weight (see page 26)

REVERSE PUNCH
(Karate)

(A) Assume a left forward stance, keeping your hips loose. (B) Block the opponent's lead hand downward with your left hand while preparing your right for the strike. (C) Twisting your hips to the left, strike your opponent in the solar plexus, simultaneously withdrawing your left hand for more power, and locking out your rear leg.

REVERSE ELBOW STRIKE
(Kung-Fu)

(1) Assume the left forward stance with your back leg bent for movement, your body erect and your hands held at medium height. (2 & 3) Pivot 180 degrees counterclockwise on your forward foot and as your right foot makes contact with the floor, execute a right reverse elbow strike. Be sure you are making contact with the point of your elbow.

Supplementary weight exercises include:

1. Bench Press (see page 18)
2. Bent Arm Laterals (see page 22)
3. Push Ups With Weight (see page 26)

REVERSE ELBOW STRIKE
(Karate)

(A) Begin by facing your opponent in a right forward stance with your fists held at medium height. (B) As your opponent attempts a left reverse punch, turn 180 degrees counterclockwise on your forward foot and (C) follow through with a left reverse elbow strike to his head.

UPPER ELBOW STRIKE
(Kung-Fu)

(1) Begin by assuming a left forward stance. (2) Slide your rear leg (the right) forward. (3) When your right foot is even with the heel of your left, lock your left leg back while simultaneously raising your right elbow in an upward striking motion and pulling back your left hand for power.

Supplementary weight exercises include:

1. Bench Press (see page 18)
2. Bent Arm Laterals (see page 22)
3. Push Ups With Weight (see page 26)
4. Standing Press (see page 28)
5. Upright Rowing (see page 30)

UPPER ELBOW STRIKE
(Karate)

(A) Assume a left forward stance. (B) Slide your right leg forward while you block your opponent's lead hand with your left hand. (C) Strike upward with your right elbow, making contact with the point of your elbow into the opponent's chin. Be sure to lock back your left leg and lower your left hand simultaneously with the elbow strike.

HORIZONTAL ELBOW STRIKE
(Kung-Fu)

(1) Begin by assuming a left forward stance. (2) Slide your right foot forward until it is even with the heel of your left foot. (3) Lock your left leg behind you (so that you are in a right forward stance) and strike outward with your right elbow, keeping the strike at about shoulder level.

1

Supplementary weight exercises include:

1. Bench Press (see page 18)
2. Bent Arm Laterals (see page 22)
3. Push Ups With Weight (see page 26)
4. Standing Press (see page 28)
5. Upright Rowing (see page 30)

HORIZONTAL ELBOW STRIKE
(Karate)

(A) Assume the left forward stance. (B) Block the opponent's strike by lowering your left fist into it, or by a rising block. (C) Hit your opponent with a horizontal elbow strike into the solar plexus after you assume a low forward stance.

A

130

U PUNCH
(Kung-Fu)

(1) Begin by assuming a left forward stance. (2) From the left forward stance, lean your weight on your left leg and simultaneously strike the opponent in the head and body. Your right hand should strike the head and your left, the body, giving a U-shaped appearance from the side. (3) Return to your original left forward stance immediately after contact.

Supplementary weight exercises include:

1. Bench Press (see page 18)
2. Bent Arm Laterals (see page 22)
3. Alternate Dumbbell Presses (see page 32)

U PUNCH
(Karate)

(A) Assume the left forward stance. (B) Putting most of your weight on your left leg, simultaneously punch the opponent's head and body, your right hand hitting the head and your left hitting the body.

OPEN HAND U STRIKE
(Kung-Fu)

(1) Begin by assuming a left forward stance. (2) Leaning most of your weight on your front leg, strike your opponent in the face with your open right hand, and in the groin with your open left hand. (3) After contact, return immediately to your original left forward stance.

Supplementary weight exercises include:

1. Bench Press (see page 18)
2. Bent Arm Laterals (see page 22)
3. Alternate Dumbbell Presses (see page 32)
4. Reverse Wrist Curls (see page 72)

OPEN HAND U STRIKE
(Karate)

(A) Assume the left forward stance. (B) Like the man on the left of the photo, strike simultaneously with both hands open to the face and groin.

TWO HAND RIB STRIKE
(Kung-Fu)

(1) Begin by assuming the left forward stance. (2) Placing most of your weight on your forward foot, swing your arms inward in a circular motion and strike your opponent on both sides of the body simultaneously. The two prominent knuckles on each fist should be making the contact. (3) Assume your original left forward stance immediately after contact.

1

Supplementary weight exercises include:

1. Bench Press (see page 18)
2. Bent Arm Laterals (see page 22)
3. Dumbbell Crossovers (see page 20)
4. Dumbbell Bicep Curls (see page 56)

TWO HAND RIB STRIKE
(Karate)

(A) Begin by assuming the left forward stance. (B) As the opponent reaches for you, move into a right forward stance (C) and strike on both sides of the ribs with the two prominent knuckles on each fist.

A

BACK KNUCKLE STRIKE
(Kung-Fu)

(1) Begin by assuming a left forward stance. (2 & 3) Slide your front foot forward while you make an outward strike with your left fist, using the two prominent knuckles on that hand as the contact points.

Supplementary weight exercises include:

1. Dumbbell Crossovers (see page 20)
2. Upright Rowing (see page 30)
3. Standing Laterals (see page 34)
4. Bent Over Laterals (see page 36)

BACK KNUCKLE STRIKE
(Karate)

(A) Assume the left forward stance. (B) Slide your front foot forward while blocking your opponent's attacking hand downward with your right hand and draw your left fist back across your chin, making ready for the strike. (C) Strike your opponent in the temple with the prominent knuckles of your left hand.

REVERSE BACK KNUCKLE STRIKE
(Kung-Fu)

(1) Begin by assuming the left forward stance. (2) Slide your right foot clockwise (to the right) until (3) it has gone a full 180 degrees, at which time the back of your right fist should strike the opponent's head. Contact should be made with the two prominent knuckles on your fist.

Supplementary weight exercises include:

1. Dumbbell Crossovers (see page 20)
2. Upright Rowing (see page 30)
3. Standing Laterals (see page 34)
4. Bent Over Laterals (see page 36)

REVERSE BACK KNUCKLE STRIKE
(Karate)

(A) Assume the right forward stance, with your right leg and right arm leading. (B) Slide your rear leg counterclockwise a full 180 degrees and cock your left arm in preparation for the strike. (C) Snap your left arm out, bringing the prominent knuckles of your left hand in contact with your opponent's temple.

ARM BREAK TECHNIQUE
(Kung-Fu)

(1) Assume a right forward stance. (2) From this position, block with your left hand and bring your right arm sharply up into the opponent's elbow. (3) Return to the right forward stance immediately after contact.

Supplementary weight exercises include:

1. Dumbbell Crossovers (see page 20)
2. Upright Rowing (see page 30)
3. Standing Laterals (see page 34)
4. Bent Over Laterals (see page 36)

ARM BREAK TECHNIQUE
(Karate)

(A) Begin by assuming a right forward stance. (B) As your opponent reaches forward, pin his hand to your chest with your left hand and ready your right arm for an upward blow. (C) Being sure you keep the opponent's hand pinned, bring your right arm up sharply, striking the opponent's elbow with your forearm.

INSIDE FOREARM BLOCK, BACK HAND COUNTER

(1 & 2) In **kung-fu,** begin in a left forward stance and execute a left inside forearm block while grasping with your right hand. (3 & 4) Maintaining your right hand grip, execute a left back hand strike. (A & B) In **karate,** begin in a left forward stance and execute a left inside forearm block while grasping the

opponent's punch with your right hand. (C & D) Maintaining your grip, execute a left back hand strike to your opponent's jaw.**Supplementary weight exercises** include Upright Rowing (see page 30), Standing Laterals (see page 34), and Bent Over Laterals (see page 36).

INSIDE FOREARM LEG
BLOCK AND BACKFIST COUNTER
(Kung-Fu)

(1) Begin by assuming a left forward stance. (2) Perform an inside forearm leg block with your left arm. (3) With the same motion, rotate your left arm upward and strike out with a backfist counter.

Supplementary weight exercises include:

1. Upright Rowing (see page 30)
2. Standing Laterals (see page 34)
3. Bent Over Laterals (see page 36)

INSIDE FOREARM LEG
BLOCK AND BACKFIST COUNTER
(Karate)

(A) Assume a left forward stance. (B) When your opponent attacks with a left front kick, you should use your left arm for an inside forearm block. (C) From here, rotate your blocking arm upward and attack with a backfist to the face of your opponent.

LUNGE PUNCH-REVERSE PUNCH
(Kung-Fu)

(1) Begin by assuming the left forward stance. (2) Slide your rear foot forward and execute a right lunge punch. (3) Immediately after making contact, throw a reverse punch into the body with your left hand.

Supplementary weight exercises include:

1. Alternate Dumbbell Press
   (see page 32)
2. Standing Press (see page 28)
3. Bench Press (see page 18)

LUNGE PUNCH-REVERSE PUNCH
(Karate)

(A) Assume a left forward stance. (B) Slide quickly into a right forward stance by executing a lunge punch with your right hand to the opponent's face. (C) Follow this up immediately with a left reverse strike to the opponent's solar plexus.

2

3

B

C

OPEN HAND BLOCK-PALM STRIKE
(Kung-Fu)

(1) Assume the left forward stance. (2) Slide your rear leg along into a right forward stance while simultaneously blocking with an open hand left block. (3) Quickly strike your opponent's chin with a right hand palm heel strike.

Supplementary weight exercises include:

1. Bench Press (see page 18)
2. Alternate Dumbbell Press (see page 32)
3. Standing Press (see page 28)
4. Dumbbell Reverse Wrist Curls (see page 72)

1

OPEN HAND BLOCK-PALM STRIKE
(Karate)

(A) Assume a left forward stance. (B) When your opponent attacks with a right reverse punch, execute a left open hand block. (C) Quickly step forward into a right forward stance, simultaneously attacking with a right palm strike to the opponent's chin.

A

RISING BLOCK-REVERSE PUNCH
(Kung-Fu)

(1) Begin by assuming the left forward stance. (2) Raise your left arm in a rising arm block. (3) Quickly counter with a right reverse punch to the left solar plexus region, while you pull your left fist back into your body.

Supplementary weight exercises include:

1. Alternate Dumbbell Press
   (see page 32)
2. Standing Press (see page 28)
3. Upright Rowing (see page 30)
4. Standing Laterals (see page 34)
5. Bench Press (see page 18)

RISING BLOCK-REVERSE PUNCH
(Karate)

(A) Assume the left forward stance. (B) When your opponent attacks with a lunge punch at your face, counter it with a left rising block. (C) Quickly follow through with a right reverse punch to your opponent's solar plexis.

PULL AND FOOTSWEEP
(Kung-Fu)

(1) Begin by assuming the left forward stance. (2) Slide your rear leg forward with the arch of your foot pointed straight ahead, and use your right hand to grab the opponent. (3) With your right leg, sweep the opponent's front leg while simultaneously pulling his body in the opposite direction.

1

Supplementary weight exercises include:

1. Lat Pull Downs On Machine (see page 42)
2. Bent Over Rowing (see page 38)
3. Dumbbell Rowing (see page 40)
4. Dumbbell Pull Overs (see page 24)
5. Barbell Bicep Curls (see page 54)
6. Squats (see pages 58-63)
7. Heel Raises (see page 78)

PULL AND FOOTSWEEP
(Karate)

(A) From the left forward stance, begin sliding your rear leg forward, while, at the same time, grabbing your opponent's sleeve. (B) Use your right leg to sweep the forward leg of your opponent vigorously, simultaneously with your pulling of the opponent's sleeve in the opposite direction. (C) Follow through with pulling your opponent off balance until he hits the ground, at which time you deliver the final attack.

A

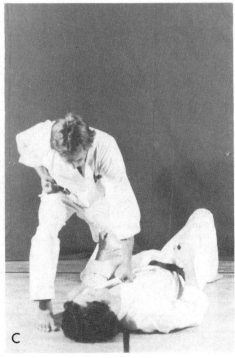

2

3

B

C

SHUFFLE CHOP COUNTER
(Kung-Fu)

(1) Begin by assuming a left forward stance. (2) Holding this position, bring your left hand up with your forearm going across the chin, in preparation for the chop strike. (3) Keeping your body straight, push off your rear foot and shuffle on your front foot as you deliver the blow. The chop strike should fall in an outward and downward direction.

Supplementary weight exercises include:

1. Tricep Push Downs On Lat Machine (see page 44)
2. French Curls With Barbell (see page 46)
3. Barbell Curl And Press (see page 48)

SHUFFLE CHOP COUNTER
(Karate)

(A) Face your opponent in a left forward stance, keeping relaxed but alert. (B) As the opponent makes a forward move, bring your front leg up and cock your striking hand across your chin. (C) Shuffle in and strike your opponent on the side of the neck with the outside blade of your hand.

ELBOW BREAK COUNTER
(Kung-Fu)

(1) Begin by assuming the left forward stance, keeping relaxed and alert. (2) Keeping your feet in position, shift your weight to the forward foot (the left, in this case) and block and grab with your right hand. (3) Leaning even further to the left, deliver a left elbow strike in a direction away from your body.

1

Supplementary weight exercises include:

1. Reverse Dips On Bench With Weight (see page 50)
2. Bomb 21 Tricep Curls (see page 52)
3. Tricep Extensions On Lat Machine (see page 45)

ELBOW BREAK COUNTER
(Karate)

(A) Assume a left forward stance, facing your opponent. (B) As your opponent attacks with a right hand lunge punch, swivel to the left, blocking and grasping your opponent's attacking arm. (C) As soon as you grasp at his wrist, strike his elbow with your forearm, executing an inward block. This will often break an arm at the elbow.

A

RIDGE-HAND COUNTER

(1) In **kung-fu,** begin in a left forward stance and block outward with your left hand. (2) Turn your hips slightly and strike with the thumb side of your right hand, being sure to tuck your thumb in toward the palm. (A) In **karate,** begin by facing your opponent in a left forward stance. (B) Grasp your opponent's right attacking arm with your left hand while (C) simultaneously delivering a ridge-hand strike to his neck. **Supplementary weight exercises** include Dumbbell Wrist Curls (see page 76), Pinch Grip Curls (see page 74), Seated Dumbbell Bicep Curls (see page 56), and Barbell Curls (see page 57).

A

LEG SWEEP TAKEDOWN AGAINST WHEEL KICK

(1 & 2) **In kung-fu,** begin from a right forward stance, slide your front foot forward and perform an inside block. (3) Keeping both hands open, scoop up with your left and thrust your right toward the opponent's face. (4) Kick your right leg out to the rear while pushing your right hand forward. (A & B) **In karate,** begin in a right forward stance, slide your front leg forward and perform an inside block. (C) Grasp your opponent's kicking leg with your left

3

4

hand while executing a right open hand strike to his face. (D) Hook your right leg behind your opponent's anchor leg and sweep backward while you push him to the ground with your right open hand strike. **Supplementary weight exercises** include Lat Pull Downs (see page 42), Tricep Extension On Lat Machine (see page 45), Hack Squats (see page 60), and Leg Curls On Machine (see page 66).

C

D

LEG SWEEP
TAKEDOWN AGAINST FRONT KICK
(Kung-Fu)

(1) Begin by assuming a left forward stance. (2) Begin sliding your rear foot forward while you make a scoop block with your right hand and drive your open left hand toward your opponent's face. (3) Hook your right leg behind the opponent's for the takedown, while pushing back with your left hand.

1

Supplementary weight exercises include:

1. Leg Curls On Machine (see page 66)
2. Barbell Bicep Curls (see page 54)
3. Front Squats (see page 63)
4. Bent Over Rowing (see page 38)

LEG SWEEP
TAKEDOWN AGAINST FRONT KICK
(Karate)

(A) As your opponent attempts a front kick, scoop his leg with your right arm and cock your left hand to protect your face. (B) Maintaining your grip on his leg, thrust your left open hand into his face and hook his anchor leg with your right leg. (C) Kick your right leg sideways and drive your opponent to the floor with your left hand.

A

FOOT SWEEP
AGAINST THE SIDE KICK
(Kung-Fu)

(1) Begin by assuming a left forward stance. (2) Perform an inside block with your left hand while you scoop upward with your right arm. (3) Maintaining your hands in these positions, perform a sweep action with your left leg.

Supplementary weight exercises include:

1. Squats (see pages 58-63)
2. One Arm Dumbbell Rowing (see page 40)
3. Seated Dumbbell Curls (see page 56)
4. Sit Ups On Bench (see page 84)

FOOT SWEEP
AGAINST THE SIDE KICK
(Karate)

(A) From a left forward stance, block your opponent's side kick with an inside block of your left hand and grasp his leg with your right. (B) Shuffle once forward so that your right leg is positioned to hook your opponent's anchor leg and grasp his shoulder with your left hand. (C) Down your opponent by sweeping your left leg and deliver a left side kick to his face, once downed.

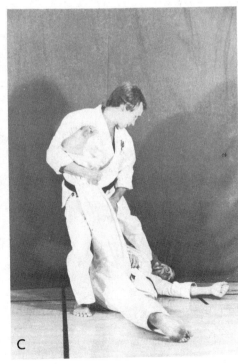

GRAB AND PUNCH
(Kung-Fu)

(1) Begin by assuming a left forward stance. (2) Placing most of your weight on your front leg, reach forward and grab your opponent's arm. (3) Pull your opponent in and deliver a reverse strike with your right fist to his body.

Supplementary weight exercises include:

1. Seated Barbell Curls (see page 57)
2. Dumbbell Wrist Curls (see page 76)
3. Pinch Grip Exercise (see page 74)
4. Barbell Bicep Curls (see page 54)

GRAB AND PUNCH
(Karate)

(A) Face your opponent in a left forward stance. (B) Grab your opponent's lead arm with your left hand. (C) Pull inward with your left, and deliver a right hand reverse punch to his solar plexus.

LEG SWEEP AGAINST LUNGE PUNCH

(1 & 2) In **kung-fu,** begin in a right forward stance, and perform an inside left palm block while swiveling clockwise at the hips. (3) Grasp your opponent's gi with your right hand. (4) Sweep back with your right leg and push forward with both hands. (A & B) In **karate,** face your opponent in a right forward stance and as he attempts a right lunge punch, perform a left inside palm

block and grab his gi with your right hand. (C & D) Sweep his front leg with your right leg and push him to the ground with both hands. **Supplementary weight exercises** include Leg Curls On Machine (see page 66), Half Squats (see page 62), Lat Pull Downs (see page 42), Reverse Dumbbell Wrist Curls (see page 72), and Heel Raises (see page 78).

DEFENSE AGAINST FULL NELSON

(1 & 2) In **kung-fu,** begin in a natural position and quickly tense your upper back muscles. (3) Make a 90-degree turn by stepping out with your right foot and execute a left back hand to the temple. (4) Immediately follow up with a right reverse punch. (A & B) In **karate,** begin in a natural stance and quickly tense your upper back muscles to prevent completion of a full nelson. (C)

Make a 90-degree turn by stepping out with your right foot and execute a left back hand strike to the temple. (D) Immediately follow up with a right reverse punch to the solar plexus. **Supplementary weight exercises** include Lat Pull Downs (see page 42), Bent Over Rowing (see page 38), Standing Press (see page 28), Dumbbell Crossovers (see page 20), and Bench Press (see page 18).

CHOP COUNTER AGAINST TACKLE
(Kung-Fu)

(1) Begin by assuming a left forward stance. (2) Step backward with your left leg. (3) Block downward with your left arm, continuing to pull back your left leg until you are in a horse stance. From the horse stance, use your right hand for a downward chop.

Supplementary weight exercises include:

1. Bomb 21 Tricep Curls (see page 52)
2. French Curls (see page 46)
3. Reverse Dips On Bench (see page 50)

CHOP COUNTER AGAINST TACKLE
(Karate)

(A) Assume a left forward stance. (B) As your opponent tries to make a tackle, step back quickly with your left foot and execute a downward left hand block. (C) Follow through with your left leg until you have reached a horse stance, at which time you perform a right hand chop down on the opponent's neck.

174

2

3

B

C

LUNGE PUNCH-HAMMER FIST COMBINATION

(1 & 2) In **kung-fu,** begin in a left forward stance, slide your rear leg forward into a right forward stance and execute a lunge punch to the face. (3) Shift into a horse stance and cock your right fist. (4) Execute a hammer fist to the groin. (A & B) In **karate,** begin in a left forward stance, slide your rear leg up

into a right forward stance and execute a lunge punch to the face. (C) Shift into a horse stance and cock your right fist. (D) Execute a right hammer fist to the groin. **Supplementary weight exercises** include the Bench Press (see page 18), Barbell Curl And Press (see page 48), Alternate Dumbbell Press (see page 32), and Push Ups With Weights (see page 26).

REVERSE CHOP COUNTER AGAINST PUNCH

(1 & 2) In **kung-fu,** begin in a left forward stance and perform an inside forearm block. (3) Turn 180 degrees counterclockwise on your left foot and cock your right arm. (4) Step into a horse stance and execute a right reverse chop. (A & B) In **karate,** face your opponent in a left forward stance and perform a left inside block to his punch. (C) Turn 180 degrees

counterclockwise on your left foot and cock your right arm. (D) Step into a horse stance and execute a right reverse chop to your opponent's jaw. **Supplementary weight exercises** include Dumbbell Crossovers (see page 20), Upright Rowing (see page 30), Standing Laterals (see page 34), and Lat Machine Tricep Pushdowns (see page 44).

KICKING

With proper training and use, the thrusting and snapping power in your legs for kicking can be transformed into an effective, if not lethal, weapon. Many different styles of karate and kung-fu rely heavily on kicking expertise as a deadly means of counterattack.

There is a great variety of kicks and, as we have mentioned earlier in this book, it is not our purpose to teach these techniques thoroughly, but rather to show you how you can increase their power when you perform them in conjunction with weight training. The kicks listed in this section represent both the simple and the advanced techniques of many different styles of karate and kung-fu, and they should give you a good cross-section view of how certain weight and stretching exercises will help you to improve them.

Since all of the kicks will use basically the same leg muscles for lifting, snapping and thrusting, a single set of supplementary exercises will be applicable to all of them. The suggested exercises, both with weights and without, are as follows:

1. All squatting exercises (see pages 58-63)
2. Leg curls (see pages 66-67)
3. Toe raises (see pages 80-81)
4. Leg raises on the extension machine (see pages 64-67)
5. All leg stretching exercises (see pages 190-201, 204-207)

SIDE KICK

(1) Begin by facing your opponent in a left forward stance with your fists held at medium height. (2) Lift your forward leg while you twist your hips inward and point the toes of your anchor foot slightly outward. (3) Deliver the kick to the midsection of your opponent by straightening your leg and thrusting the outside blade of your foot at the target.

SKIPPING SIDE KICK

(1) Begin by facing your opponent in a right forward stance with your fists held at medium height. (2) Bring your rear leg forward along the floor so that it touches the heel of your front leg, and then raise your forward leg by bending your knee. (3) Deliver a side kick to the head of your opponent, being sure to use the outside blade of your kicking foot as the striking point.

1

CIRCLE BACK KICK

(1) Begin by facing your opponent in a left forward stance with your fists held at medium height. (2) Move your left leg slightly back and pivot on it so that your body quickly swings around to the right while you lift your right leg in preparation for the kick. You should be sure to keep your eyes fixed on the target by looking over your right shoulder. (3) Execute a side kick to the opponent's chest area.

1

2

3

2

3

1

FRONT THRUST KICK

(1) Begin by facing your opponent in a left forward stance with your fists held at medium height in a ready position. (2) Quickly bring your rear leg forward bending it so

2

3

that your knee is at chest level. (3) Thrust the heel of your foot into your opponent's midsection by straightening your leg, and (4) follow through by straightening your knee completely.

4

1

FRONT SNAP KICK

(1) Begin by assuming a left forward stance with your fists held at medium height. (2) Bring your rear leg forward, bending it at the knee and (3) snap your foot out to hit the target with the ball of your

2

3

foot. (4) Immediately upon contact, bend your foot back beneath your knee. From here, you may either step your kicking foot forward or back to its original position.

4

STRETCHING AND NON-WEIGHT RESISTANT EXERCISES

The exercises contained in this chapter are important to any serious martial artist's training program. It should be included in one's daily training schedule, particularly before and after workouts with weights. Kung-Fu and Karate masters believed strongly that it is more vital to add one inch to the length of a muscle than to add five inches to its size. The exercises in the subsequent chapter will accomplish that end.

CARDIOVASCULAR NON-WEIGHT TRAINING ROUTINE

1. Run between half a mile and a mile. Work against the clock for speed.
2. Include all types of Push Ups (see pages 208-213) with 3 sets of 10 to 30 repetitions each.
3. Include all types of Sit Ups (see pages 82-5) with 4 sets of 15 to 40 repetitions each.
4. Include Leg Raises (see page 206) with 4 sets of 15 to 40 repetitions.
5. Include Single Leg Squats (see page 198) with 4 sets of 10 to 15 repetitions.
6. Include Bunny Hops (see page 202) with 4 sets of 10 to 15 repetitions.
7. Include Lower Trunk Extensions (see pages 201) with 4 sets of 10 to 15 repetitions each.
8. Include tumbling or gymnastic exercises.

This program is designed for daily use or from five to six days per week.

GENERAL HINTS FOR
CARDIOVASCULAR NON-WEIGHT TRAINING ROUTINE

1. Running (run, don't jog)
2. Run against the clock to improve on speed.
3. Stretch before and after running.
4. Cool off slowly and keep moving.
5. Push ups are done strictly, with high repetitions.
6. Leg raises: Keep legs straight and concentrate on lower abdomen.
7. Sit ups: Concentrate on contracting abdomen and do not bounce up.
8. Gymnastics: Perform some sort of daily tumbling to improve on agility, coordination and balance.
9. Single Leg Squats: Do not touch the floor with the extended foot or hands. Single legged squats are important in developing strength and balance, an important factor in good kicking.
10. Bunny hops: Jump with as much thrust as you can to improve explosive power.
11. Perform all exercises in this program daily or five to six days a week.

SIDE SPLITS STRETCHING HEAD FORWARD

(1) Begin the exercise by leaning forward, supporting your weight with both of your hands and spreading your legs apart to the side. (2) Ease your body down slowly until you are in a sitting position. (3) With your trunk leaning slightly forward, grab your ankles with your hands. (4) From this position, bend forward until your head touches the floor.

It is important to note that a beginner will not probably be able to do this exercise without practice. Don't push yourself, but go as far as you can and gradually work up to perfecting the exercise. It will take time.

SIDE SPLITS ALTERNATING HEAD TO THE SIDE

(1) Begin in the sitting position with your legs extended straight out and your feet spread wide apart. (2) Turn your trunk slightly to the left and bend down until you touch your left knee with your head (3). Be sure to keep your legs spread and flat on the floor at all times. Alternate this exercise from your left to your right.

ONE LEGGED SIDE SPLITS

(1) Begin in the sitting position with your right leg pulled in toward your trunk and your right foot placed flat on the floor. Keep your left leg spread at a 90 degree angle with your right and be sure it is flat on the floor. (2) With the palms of your hands placed flat on the floor, begin slowly to bend your trunk forward until (3) your head touches your knee.

FRONT SPLITS

(1) Begin in a standing position, facing straight ahead with your legs slightly apart. (2) Slide your right leg forward, keeping it straight while your left leg bends from its stationary position. (3) Achieve the front split slowly by placing your hands at your sides and flat on the floor. When the split is completed, the rear leg (your left, in this case) should be as straight as possible and as flat as possible on the floor.

Repeat this exercise the desired number of times before reversing your legs.

SITTING STRETCH

(1) Begin in the sitting position and hold the soles of your feet together with your hands. (2 & 3) Bend forward very slowly until your head touches your feet.

HAND BRIDGE

(1) Begin this exercise in the prone position with your feet placed flat on the floor against your buttocks. Be sure they are placed about shoulder width apart. Place your hands flat on the floor with your fingers pointed back toward your shoulders. (2 & 3) Arch your back upward and push off with your legs and hands into a bridge.

TWO LEGGED FRONT STRETCH

(1) Begin by assuming a sitting position with your legs extended together and flat on the floor. (2) Lean forward and grab the bottoms of both feet with your hands. (3 & 4) Keeping your legs straight, bend slowly forward until your head reaches near your knees.

THE HURDLERS SPLITS

(1) Begin by assuming the hurdler's split position, sitting on the floor with your left leg extended flat in front of you. Your back leg should be bent. (2) Twist to your left and touch your toes with your right hand. (3) Then twist your trunk as far to the right as possible. (4) Complete the cycle by touching your left foot with your right hand again. Repeat this process, alternating your left and right leg extended out.

ONE LEGGED SQUATS

(1) Assume a standing position with your arms at your sides. (2) Raise your arms straight out to the side and lift your right leg until it is extended straight away from you. (3 & 4) Being sure to keep your right

leg extended, squat down on your left leg. Refrain from touching the floor. (5 & 6) From the squat position, return to the starting position, being sure to keep your right leg extended. You may alternate this exercise on each leg.

STANDING FRONT BENDS

(1) Begin in a standing position with your feet together and your arms at your sides. (2-4) Being sure to keep your legs straight, bend forward until your head touches against the front of your knee and your hands grasp the backs of your calves.

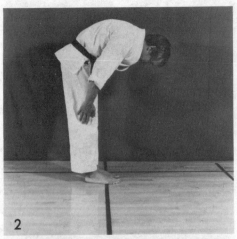

ALTERNATE LEG STRETCH

(1) Begin in a squat position and extend your right leg straight out to the right. Your left foot should be flat on the floor. (2) Being sure to keep your feet in exactly the same place on the floor, bend your knees and shift your body until you have alternated to the other side. Your hands may be used in this exercise to grasp your knees or ankles.

BUNNY HOPS

(1) Begin by assuming a squat position with your hands clasped behind your back. Be sure you are squatting on your toes. (2 & 3) From this position, thrust yourself into the air as high as you can go. Be sure you thrust yourself slightly forward each time. Repeat this process.

1

ALTERNATE STANDING BENDS

(1) Begin in a standing position with your feet together and your hands at your sides. (2 & 3) Keeping your legs straight, bend over to the left until the knuckles of your fists touch the floor. Return to the original standing position and repeat the process bending to the right side. Each movement should be done on a three count basis.

1

2

3

2

3

TWO MAN SPLITS

(1) Begin in the split position with your legs extended flat on the floor. Have your partner place his hands on your shoulders. (2 & 3) Allow your partner to push you slowly forward until your head touches the floor. Be sure your hands are grasping toward your ankles at all times.

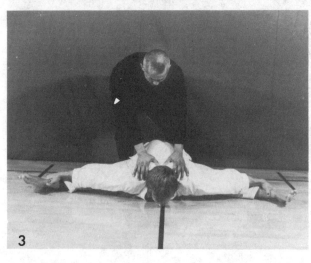

TWO MAN ALTERNATE LEG STRETCH

(1) Begin in the split position facing your training partner, who is in the same position. Place your feet against those of your partner and grasp your partner's wrists. (2) From this position, pull backward until your back is flat on the floor. (3) Allow your partner to pull backward to his side. Alternate back and forth in this way.

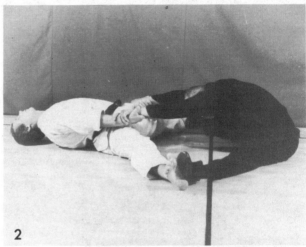

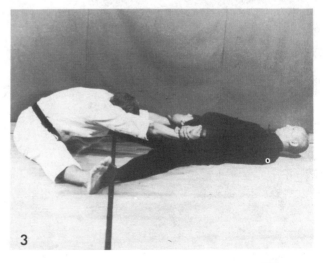

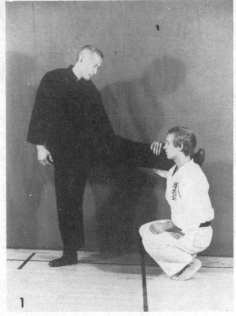

1

2

3

SIDE KICK LEG RAISES

(1) Begin in the standing position and have your partner assume a squatting position. Place your left leg on the right shoulder of your partner. (2 & 3) With your anchor foot pointing away from your partner, bend your trunk toward your partner as he stands up slowly. Be sure to keep your stretching leg straight at all times.

FRONT KICK LEG RAISES

(1) From the standing position, face your partner and place your right leg on his left shoulder. Be sure your partner places his hands on your knee to keep it locked and straight. (2 & 3) Bend forward slowly and grasp the elevated foot with your right hand. Be sure to keep the elevated leg straight at all times. Alternate legs when you are finished.

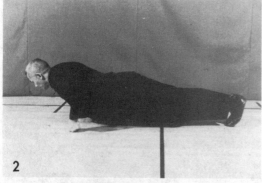

PUSH UPS
ON KNUCKLES

(1) Begin by assuming the classic push-up position, only placing your weight on the knuckles of your fists. Be sure your back is straight, your feet are close together and your fists are about shoulder width apart on the floor. (2 & 3) Inhale as you lower your body until it touches the floor. (4) Push up until your return to the starting position, exhaling as you go and keeping your back straight.

PUSH UPS ON FINGERS

(1) Begin in the normal push up position, with your weight resting on your outstretched thumb and forefinger. (Beginners should stretch out all five fingers until they become proficient enough to do this exercise on only two fingers). (2 & 3) Inhale as you lower your body until your chest touches the floor. (4) Exhale as you push up back into starting position. Be sure to keep your back straight when doing all push ups.

WRIST PUSH UPS

(1) Begin by assuming the regular push up position, only be sure you support your weight on the backs of your wrists. (2-4) Inhale as you slowly lower your body until

your chest touches the floor. Be sure you are keeping your back straight. (5) Push up from this position, exhaling as you go, until you reach the original starting position.

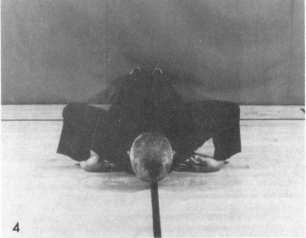

ONE ARM
PUSH UPS ON
THE KNUCKLES

(1) Begin in a push up position, with your legs spread behind you at about shoulder-and-a-half width. Rest all of your weight on the knuckles of your right fist while you anchor your left hand behind your buttocks. (2 & 3) Lower your body slowly as you inhale until your chest touches the floor. (4) Exhale as you push yourself up with your right hand until you reach the original starting position. Alternate arms when you have completed the necessary number of repetitions.

ONE HAND FINGER PUSH UP

(1) Begin in the push up position, with your legs spread about shoulder-and-a-half width behind you. Place all of your weight on the outstretched fingers of your right hand and anchor your left hand to your thigh. (2 & 3) Inhale as you lower your body until your chest touches the floor. (4) Pause slightly and exhale as you push up with your right hand until you are in the original starting position. Alternate arms when you have completed the necessary number of repetitions.

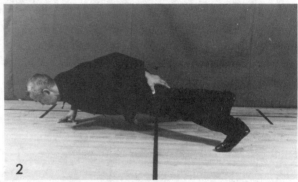

213

HAND STAND

(1) Begin by assuming the squatting position and concentrate. (2) Lean forward and place your hands on the floor. (3 & 4) Roll forward slightly, supporting your weight on your hands with your knees resting on your elbows until your head touches the floor. (5) Smoothly push your legs upward while, at the same time, you push your whole body up with your arms. (6) From this hand stand position, roll forward on the back of your neck, being sure to tuck your knees into your body.

214

2

3

5

6

STRETCHING ROUTINE TO BE DONE DAILY

Single Stretching (without partner)
1. Front splits
2. Side splits
3. Single leg splits
4. Head to knee
5. Head to floor/side split
6. Bent leg/head to toe
7. Bridging back bend
8. Hurdlers stretch
9. Standing alternate, fist touching floor

Double Stretching (with a partner)
1. Front kick stretch
2. Side kick stretch
3. Side splits head to floor
4. Two man front stretching holding wrists

In performing stretching exercises, be sure to start gradually to avoid pulling a tendon or ligament in the leg and groin area. Perform stretching as often as possible.

MUSCLE LISTINGS AND FUNCTIONS

This section is designed to show you a detailed reference source by which you might better understand the function of your muscles and their location. The muscles are offered in their medical Latin terminology, but it should be simple to relate them to the exercise from which they benefit.

A serious student of power training would be well advised to become familiar with this section and with the anatomy charts, as they provide an excellent supplement to the practical aspects of the weight training program.

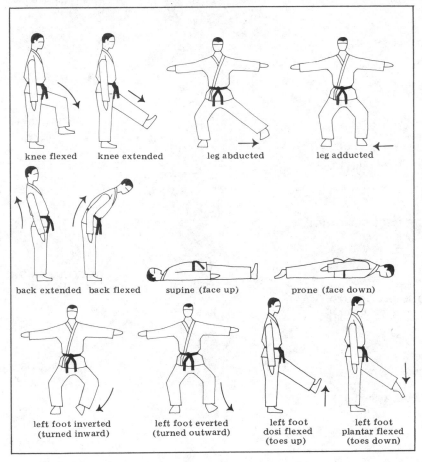

knee flexed   knee extended   leg abducted   leg adducted

back extended   back flexed   supine (face up)   prone (face down)

left foot inverted (turned inward)   left foot everted (turned outward)   left foot dosi flexed (toes up)   left foot plantar flexed (toes down)

The diagrams above are intended to help your understanding of some of the terms which appear in the following section. Each diagram should illustrate the meaning of the word below it and clarify those words as they appear in the subsequent text.

FRONT VIEW

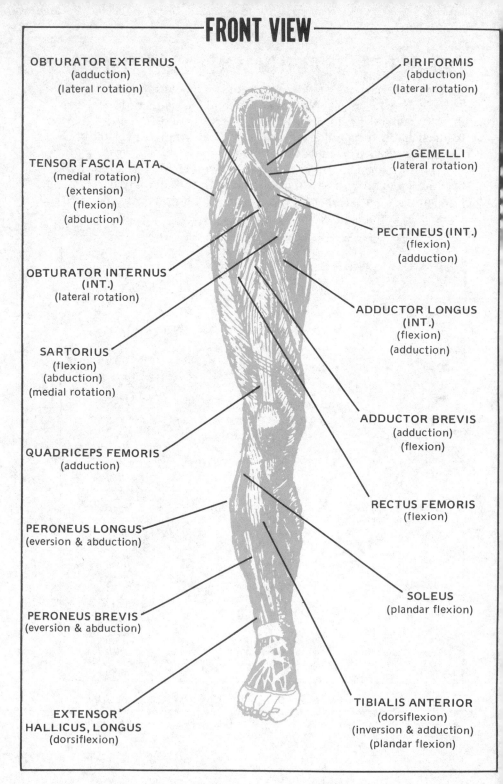

OBTURATOR EXTERNUS
(adduction)
(lateral rotation)

PIRIFORMIS
(abduction)
(lateral rotation)

GEMELLI
(lateral rotation)

TENSOR FASCIA LATA
(medial rotation)
(extension)
(flexion)
(abduction)

PECTINEUS (INT.)
(flexion)
(adduction)

OBTURATOR INTERNUS
(INT.)
(lateral rotation)

ADDUCTOR LONGUS
(INT.)
(flexion)
(adduction)

SARTORIUS
(flexion)
(abduction)
(medial rotation)

ADDUCTOR BREVIS
(adduction)
(flexion)

QUADRICEPS FEMORIS
(adduction)

RECTUS FEMORIS
(flexion)

PERONEUS LONGUS
(eversion & abduction)

SOLEUS
(plandar flexion)

PERONEUS BREVIS
(eversion & abduction)

EXTENSOR
HALLICUS, LONGUS
(dorsiflexion)

TIBIALIS ANTERIOR
(dorsiflexion)
(inversion & adduction)
(plandar flexion)

REAR VIEW

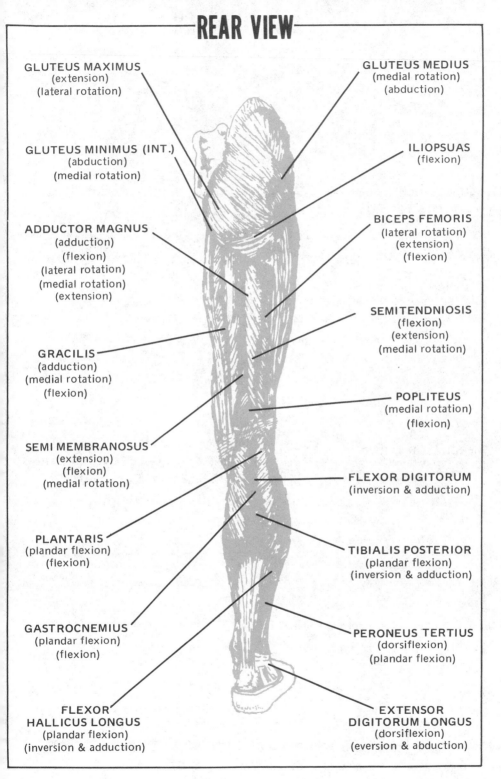

GLUTEUS MAXIMUS
(extension)
(lateral rotation)

GLUTEUS MEDIUS
(medial rotation)
(abduction)

GLUTEUS MINIMUS (INT.)
(abduction)
(medial rotation)

ILIOPSUAS
(flexion)

ADDUCTOR MAGNUS
(adduction)
(flexion)
(lateral rotation)
(medial rotation)
(extension)

BICEPS FEMORIS
(lateral rotation)
(extension)
(flexion)

SEMITENDNIOSIS
(flexion)
(extension)
(medial rotation)

GRACILIS
(adduction)
(medial rotation)
(flexion)

POPLITEUS
(medial rotation)
(flexion)

SEMI MEMBRANOSUS
(extension)
(flexion)
(medial rotation)

FLEXOR DIGITORUM
(inversion & adduction)

PLANTARIS
(plandar flexion)
(flexion)

TIBIALIS POSTERIOR
(plandar flexion)
(inversion & adduction)

GASTROCNEMIUS
(plandar flexion)
(flexion)

PERONEUS TERTIUS
(dorsiflexion)
(plandar flexion)

**FLEXOR
HALLICUS LONGUS**
(plandar flexion)
(inversion & adduction)

**EXTENSOR
DIGITORUM LONGUS**
(dorsiflexion)
(eversion & abduction)

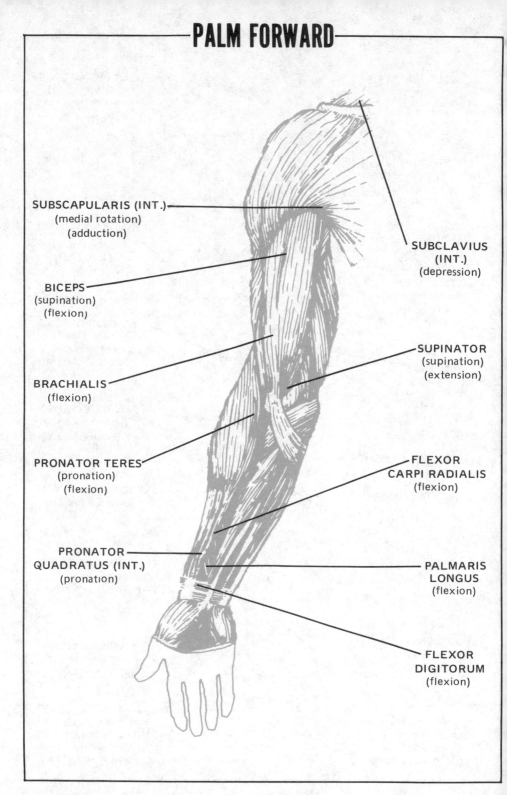

SUBSCAPULARIS (INT.)
(medial rotation)
(adduction)

SUBCLAVIUS
(INT.)
(depression)

BICEPS
(supination)
(flexion)

SUPINATOR
(supination)
(extension)

BRACHIALIS
(flexion)

PRONATOR TERES
(pronation)
(flexion)

FLEXOR
CARPI RADIALIS
(flexion)

PRONATOR
QUADRATUS (INT.)
(pronation)

PALMARIS
LONGUS
(flexion)

FLEXOR
DIGITORUM
(flexion)

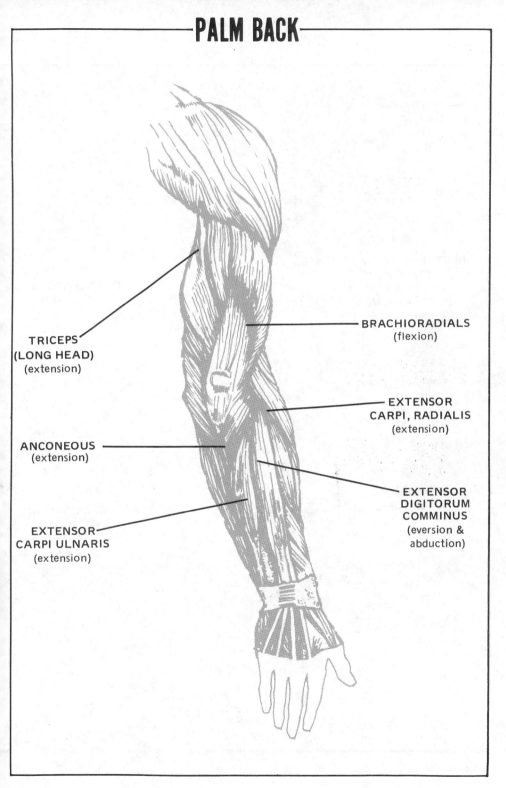

**TRICEPS
(LONG HEAD)**
(extension)

BRACHIORADIALS
(flexion)

**EXTENSOR
CARPI, RADIALIS**
(extension)

ANCONEOUS
(extension)

**EXTENSOR
DIGITORUM
COMMINUS**
(eversion &
abduction)

**EXTENSOR
CARPI ULNARIS**
(extension)

FRONT VIEW

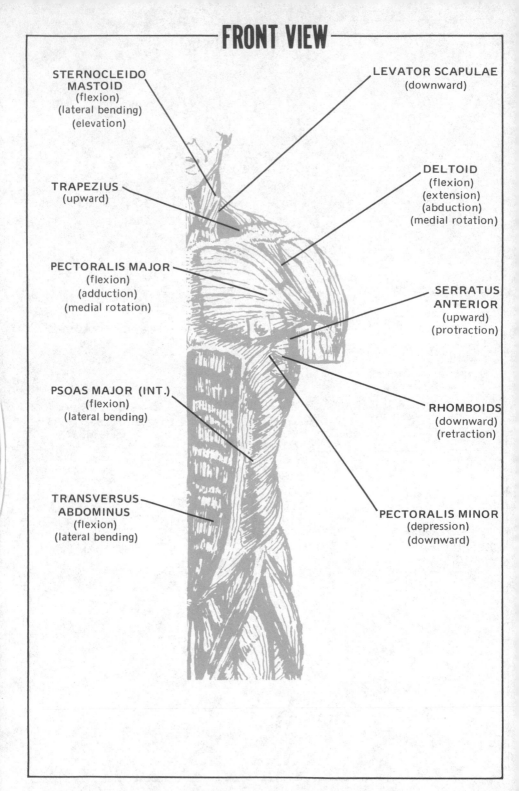

STERNOCLEIDO
MASTOID
(flexion)
(lateral bending)
(elevation)

LEVATOR SCAPULAE
(downward)

DELTOID
(flexion)
(extension)
(abduction)
(medial rotation)

TRAPEZIUS
(upward)

PECTORALIS MAJOR
(flexion)
(adduction)
(medial rotation)

SERRATUS
ANTERIOR
(upward)
(protraction)

PSOAS MAJOR (INT.)
(flexion)
(lateral bending)

RHOMBOIDS
(downward)
(retraction)

TRANSVERSUS
ABDOMINUS
(flexion)
(lateral bending)

PECTORALIS MINOR
(depression)
(downward)

REAR VIEW

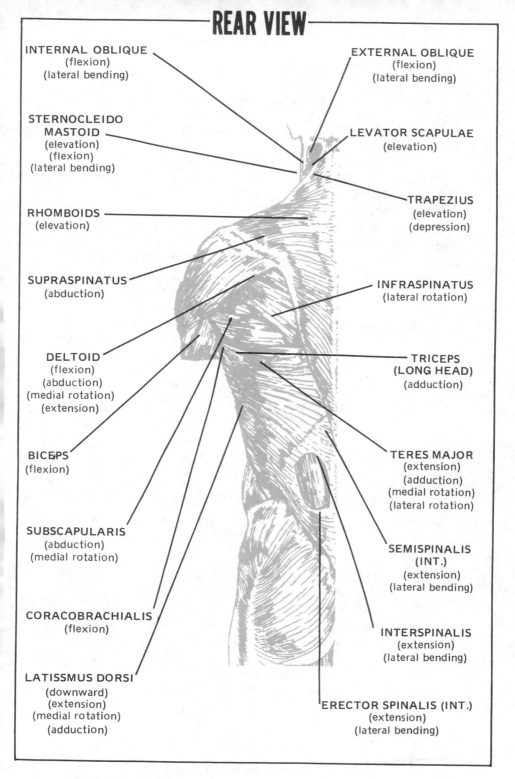

INTERNAL OBLIQUE
(flexion)
(lateral bending)

EXTERNAL OBLIQUE
(flexion)
(lateral bending)

**STERNOCLEIDO
MASTOID**
(elevation)
(flexion)
(lateral bending)

LEVATOR SCAPULAE
(elevation)

TRAPEZIUS
(elevation)
(depression)

RHOMBOIDS
(elevation)

SUPRASPINATUS
(abduction)

INFRASPINATUS
(lateral rotation)

DELTOID
(flexion)
(abduction)
(medial rotation)
(extension)

**TRICEPS
(LONG HEAD)**
(adduction)

BICEPS
(flexion)

TERES MAJOR
(extension)
(adduction)
(medial rotation)
(lateral rotation)

SUBSCAPULARIS
(abduction)
(medial rotation)

**SEMISPINALIS
(INT.)**
(extension)
(lateral bending)

CORACOBRACHIALIS
(flexion)

INTERSPINALIS
(extension)
(lateral bending)

LATISSMUS DORSI
(downward)
(extension)
(medial rotation)
(adduction)

ERECTOR SPINALIS (INT.)
(extension)
(lateral bending)

Bibliography

Cooper, Kenneth, M.D., *Aerobics*. New York, New York: M. Evans and Co., Inc. 1968

Clarke, Harrison H., *Application of Measurement to Health and Physical Education*. Englewood Cliffs, New Jersey: Prentice-Hall, Inc., (fourth printing) 1964

Fallon, Michael, and Saunders, Jim, *Muscle Building For Beginners*. New York, New York: Arco Publishing Co., Inc. 1970

Gray, Henry, F.R.S., *Anatomy of the Human Body*. Philadelphia, Pennsylvania: Lea & Febiger, (twenty-seventh printing) 1959

Loken, Newton C., and Willoughby, Roger J., *Complete Book of Gymnastics*. Englewood Cliffs, New Jersey: Prentice-Hall, Inc., (second edition) 1967

Sipes, Chuck, *Training For Strength*. Stockton, California: Sipes Publishing 1969

SUGGESTED PERIODICALS

MUSCLE BUILDER/POWER
21100 Erwin St., Woodland Hills, Ca.

SHAPE UP
21100 Erwin St., Woodland Hills, Ca.

STRENGTH AND HEALTH
P.O. Box 1707, York, Pa.

MUSCULAR DEVELOPMENT
P.O. Box 1707, York, Pa.

IRON MAN
P.O. Box 10, Alliance, Nebraska

MUSCLE TRAINING
1665 Utica Ave., Brooklyn, N.Y.